Anni Sennov

The Crystal Human
and the Crystallization Process
Part II

About the Body Crystallization Phase and Children/Adolescents of the New Time

good adventures publishing

The Crystal Human and the Crystallization Process Part II
© 2010-11, Anni Sennov and Good Adventures Publishing

Font setting: Palatino Linotype
Layout: Carsten Sennov - www.good-adventures.com
Cover design: Michael Bernth - www.monovoce.dk
Drawings: Agnes Männik - www.oledkohal.com
Illustrations: Anni Sennov - www.annisennov.eu

Original title in Danish: Krystalmennesket & Krystalliseringsprocessen
Translated into English by: Pernille Kienle of Absolute Translations &
Editing - www.absolutetranslations.dk

ISBN 978-87-92549-07-5

Acknowledgments

I would like to thank everyone who has contributed to this book with their personal Crystallization stories. It takes courage to share your own personal experiences with others and, in particular, with strangers whom you may never meet in real life.

If you would like to contact one or more of the Aura Mediators who work with AuraTransformation™, and who contributed with their stories to this book, you can find the contact information for some of them on the website below. Alternatively, please contact the Aura Mediator Instructor™ in your country.

www.auratransformation.eu

You will find my contact information at the end of the book.

I would also like to thank the Estonian Aura Mediator™, Agnes Männik, for her fun way of illustrating several of the chapters in the book. In my opinion, Agnes' drawings speak a clear language of their own.

Please note:

There are a multitude of different consciousness-expanding methods around the world that, each in their own way, aim at increasing the consciousness in the aura and/or the body.

In this book I have chosen to refer to AuraTransformation™ only, which is the consciousness-expanding method I am personally most familiar with as this method was developed by me.

It is therefore up to you, the reader, to become acquainted with other methods that inspire you.

This book refers to selected planet energies within our solar system. If this knowledge is beyond your normal conceptual field, please do not despair as this only happens a few times in the book!

In the cases contained in 'The Crystal Human and the Crystallization Process Part I' and 'The Crystal Human and the Crystallization Process Part II', several Aura Mediators™, instructors and clients mention their personal experience with various health products. These statements are based on each individual's personal experience. You will have to create your own experience and not rely too much on other people's personal experiences in connection with your personal Crystallization Process.

Neither the manufacturers, who are not aware of the publication of these two books and the effect their products may have in relation to a Body Crystallization, nor I or Good Adventures Publishing can be held responsible for the effect the mentioned products have in relation to your individual Crystallization Process.

Preface

The journey in taking the two books *'The Crystal Human and the Crystallization Process Part I'* and *'The Crystal Human and the Crystallization Process Part II'* from the original Danish version into English has been a lengthy, interesting and challenging one for all those involved in the process.sdfsdf

The Danish translator was given a remit of endeavouring to keep the style of writing as close to the original, and to Anni's own written style, as possible. While this was successfully achieved, the end result was not necessarily a document that would be experienced as either fluid or cohesive in the English language. Subsequent reviews of the two books have endeavoured to 'Englishify' them and make it a little easier on the eyes of native English (or American) speakersl.

The reader may still experience *'The Crystal Human and the Crystallization Process Part I'* and *'The Crystal Human and the Crystallization Process Part II'* as a little heavy and complicated to read in places and it has been an intentional decision to leave the books as such. For each of us involved in the translation and review of the books, we have experienced energy and magic at work, through the words that Anni has written. It was decided that retaining the integrity of this 'energy in action' was more valuable than arriving at an elegant piece of writing. Whilst Anni is known for her writing skill and fluency in Danish, this does not translate equally well into English. Her writing (and her speaking), is direct, to the point and information rich. The reader is therefore encouraged to stay with information being conveyed, rather than become involved in whether the wording or phrasing sounds 'right' or 'English'. When information is accessed from Source, the energy that works through words is often more important than the wording itself.

Working with the material provoked, induced, and stimulated crystallisation symptoms within each of us involved, and at times these were a little 'challenging'. Working towards our own individual crystallisation is however, very important, for the smooth integration of this energy into our collective experience on Mother Earth in the run up to, through 2012 and beyond. We hope and wish for you a wonderfully transforming experience reading the two books, and at the very least to finish them feeling as if you had certainly learned something new.

June McGuire
Management Consultant and Holistic Therapist

Content

INTRODUCTION

My purpose in writing the two books *'The Crystal Human and the Crystallization Process Part I'* and *'The Crystal Human and the Crystallization Process Part II'* is to outline and explain to my readers, in a tangible way, what it is like to live with and within the Crystal Energy of the New Time; that is to say with Spirit fully or partially integrated into your body and your everyday life. I will also provide some insight into how the Spirit makes its way into our bodies and about those measures that are appropriate to ensure a balanced fusion of body and spirit.

To live with the Spirit fully or partially integrated into your body is a state that everyone, who passes the transition from the Indigo Energy of the 4th dimension to the Crystal Energy of the 5th dimension, will experience at some point in their lives. *'The Crystal Human and the Crystallization Process Part I'* and *'The Crystal Human and the Crystallization Process Part II'* are therefore directed at anyone with an interest in the Crystal Energy. They are also directed at all aura-transformed adults as well as those who are considering an AuraTransformation™, because an AuraTransformation™ leads individuals from the Soul Energy through the Indigo Energy into the Crystal Energy where their Body Crystallization is activated when the time is right.

Many books describe Spiritual Energy as a pure state of being, of a non-physical nature, with which we as humans can connect, through for example meditation and healing. By connecting with this pure state of being, which many choose to call our Higher Selves, we obtain direct contact with our pure spiritual consciousness outside our bodies. This, however, requires us to be at Soul level with our consciousness, which aura-transformed individuals and the Indigo and Crystal Children of today are not. Instead, they are spiritual beings, which for Crystal Humans means that they have their own truth and divine spark, as well as their earthly life missions, deeply hidden within the cell structure of their bodies.

Up until the summer of 1996 when my aura was transformed with the help of a good friend of mine, and without either one of us knowing beforehand what this would entail, I was in touch with my Spiritual Energy almost daily, i.e. my Higher Self, through either healing, meditation or channelling.

From around 2005, however, those energy tools became unnecessary in my life, as I was able instead to just close my eyes or sit quietly by myself with my eyes wide open, without focusing on anything in particular, whenever I felt the need to recharge or gather my thoughts. It also became easier for me to find the solution to various questions in my life when I needed an immediate answer. Simply by focusing on an instant calm within my body, the answers I sought literally popped out of my system. And it still works like that for me.

The difference between 1996 and today is simply that my Spiritual Energy is now a fully integrated part of my body. My aura is very close to my body, which is why I no longer need to travel far outside my body into the outermost aura layers whenever I wish to connect with my Spiritual Energy. This saves a lot of time and effort and has given me so much energy in my everyday life - energy to do the things I want, rather than having to set aside a certain amount of time every day to quietly connect with my inner self for directions on which way to go in life and where to turn next.

If you have a busy life like I do with several children living at home, a wonderful husband and an interesting job, each with great opportunities for development, it is undeniably challenging to find sufficient time in the daily routine to nurture the Spirit as a separate part of your life and personality. It is therefore extremely liberating when your body, mind and Spirit speak the same language in every way, without having to solve any internal conflict before clearly stating your opinion to the outside world on a given topic.

Whether I use my gut feeling or my intuition, or whether I check the feeling in my big toe, I always get the same answer because the Crystal

Energy has worked itself into every part of my body and my aura and therefore into my entire system.

Nowadays for me meditation, healing and other forms of personal energy balancing work are still very enjoyable and relaxing ways to bring calm, clarity, balance and perspective, and I still enjoy this from time to time. However this only gives me a feeling of having slept for a few more hours at night and does not give my system any extraordinary kick at all. On the other hand, I get a kick at a physical level on a daily basis when I act out my ideas and succeed in doing things.

During many years of work - firstly with astrology, followed by healing and then AuraTransformation™ and clairvoyance - I have encountered many interesting, spiritually seeking individuals who, through various kinds of energy work, have worked intensively and exclusively with a focus on the spiritual aspects of life. In my eyes however, the price of this pure spiritual focus has often been that they were forced to move their consciousness focus away from the physical world, and consequently away from their physical bodies and daily lives. The majority of those people have therefore ended up in situations where they lack awareness of their everyday lives regarding their finances, work, home, family, friends, raising children and relationships, if they have indeed been able to maintain a relationship.

Having a thorough knowledge of your Higher Self, and therefore your own spiritual and consciousness potential, is always good and on par with knowing your body very well, i.e. knowing your body's strengths and weaknesses. But why even remove the body consciousness, which is the only physical tool we as humans possess to change external circumstances in our lives and our environment as a whole? After all, the body is a visible, physical manifestation of man's spiritual potential in this earthly universe, so why disallow our body's worth? The body represents our physical mobility, and the Earth is precisely where we are expected to live our current lives and where we are supposed to express ourselves in relation to each other.

Rather than applying either/or solutions in our lives, where we as humans both act as and perceive ourselves as pure spiritual beings or as earthly individuals, we must combine the two worlds by helping the Spirit enter into our bodies. This will allow the Spirit to gain a foothold in our physical reality which fully matches the fundamental structure of the Crystal Energy, and that is how the spiritual and more dense material part of us can meet as one sphere in our body to work together with each other - a condition that allows things to work for us at various levels simultaneously, not just the physical or the Spiritual level.

The fusion of the body and the Spirit can be activated in earnest if a person undergoes an AuraTransformation™. Through this, we change from being non-autonomous Soul consciousness beings to autonomous and auto-didactic Indigo and Crystal Individuals. As such, we may have one or more specific missions in respect to our earthly lives, which we are expected to act out, and in which we have the freedom or free will to choose the path(s) to that goal. This is in huge contrast to a life at Soul level where everybody has been subject to a general, common consciousness similar to that of many animals but where Soul Individuals, as opposed to animals, are here in order to learn something new and to become wiser and more intelligent in different areas. At Soul level the intention was indeed for humans to acquire knowledge consisting of insight, understanding and development and furthermore integrating foreign energies with a view to possibly cooperating with those energies.

At first an AuraTransformation™ ties our pure spiritual consciousness from the outermost aura to our bodies where the energy takes form as a combined balancing and protecting energy body. In this way, our Spiritual Energy becomes visible to others through our personal charisma. Through an AuraTransformation™ the foundation is laid for directing a large part of the pure spiritual consciousness from our auras into our physical bodies. This is called the Crystallization Process and can be a very time-consuming process.

There are countless different consciousness-expanding methods around the world, which, each in their own way, aim at increasing consciousness in the aura and the body, either simultaneously or separately. Among these methods are EMF Balancing Technique® (Electromagnetic Field Balancing), DNA Activation, Accelerating DNA Recoding Process, often combined with Multi-Dimensional Keys of Compassion, and more. Since I know little about these methods, however, I have chosen to exclusively refer to AuraTransformation™ in my two books, as that is the consciousness-expanding method that I am personally most familiar with. I leave it up to you, the reader, to learn more about the aforementioned methods, or similar methods, should you feel inspired to do so.

In all its simplicity, the Body Crystallization Process aims to combine our spiritual consciousness and spiritual power with our physical aspects and, once this has happened, it will be much easier for us to fulfill our life mission. As such, we become more mobile at the physical, spiritual, psychological and mental levels, and it becomes easier for us to adjust to our environment or seek alternatives if situations are not working for us.

You see, Crystal Humans of the New Time don't mind making crucial changes in either their everyday lives or their lives in general in order to gain ultimate balance. They always work hard to reach their goals while making every effort to avoid imbalance in their lives. On the other hand, they may take a very direct approach towards those who are not making an adequate contribution to finding a balanced solution to a given problem. When this happens, Crystal Humans are able to completely exclude those individuals from their lives and thoughts, and this can just as easily happen within the framework of family, friends and work. When Crystal Humans are confronted with injustice, backstabbing and ignorance, etc. they have no problem facing up to the individual(s) behind the smear campaign, and they have no problem going public with their discontent, since they play with open cards all the way and have nothing to hide from the outside world.

Only by letting the Spirit enter into the core of the matter and the physical substance, can we as humans increase the frequency in the heaviest and densest earthly and human energy layers, where everything is about survival, physicalisation and materialism.

This is knowledge that all Crystal Humans possess deep down at cell level. This is also why they realize that, if they are to succeed with their life mission, they must work hard to get to the bottom and clean out all dense, obdurate, physical energies and obstacles – at first within their auras – and then within their bodies and their immediate environment.

During the AuraTransformation™, all emotional imbalances are transformed and thereby completely disappear from the aura. These imbalances will therefore not interfere when you let go of any old physical memories deep down at cell level in connection with your Body Crystallization.

The Spirit should not integrate physical matter so quickly, however, that there is a risk that your body will perish or physically break down and in its hurry, the cell structure loses its physical coding and is unable to hold itself together. If the cell structure loses its physical coding, there is indeed a risk of cell dysplasia, which, in extreme cases, can develop into for example cancer or immunodeficiency disorders. It is therefore vital to take extra care of our physical bodies while the Crystallization Process, and in particular the Crystallization of the body, takes place.

You see, neither our physical body nor our physical planet is able to adjust quickly to new and unfamiliar circumstances. Not even if we try to support the process by sending out lots of positive thoughts. It takes so much longer to carry out any development, whether spiritual or technological, at a physical level than it does at a Spiritual level. For example with technological development, it is nowadays common for people to disassociate mentally from something if development happens too fast. Unfortunately, many people also develop physical allergies to for example electro-magnetic frequencies from PCs and mobile phones, which now must be considered an integral part of modern society. Many people have an almost similar reaction in connection with spiritual development, although in that case, their 'allergies' are of a more mental nature.

For me personally, the Crystallization Phase of my body represented an extremely difficult time health-wise, as I became seriously ill with asthmatic eczema for the second time in my life. This went on for several months at the end of 2003, until I got so sick and my skin was so damaged, that I agreed to receive large amounts of cortisone treatment, with the slight hope of holding together my physical body. I was unaccustomed to consuming chemically produced medication and it really compromised my personal values and beliefs at the time. However, I quickly came to realize that in this particular instance, the medication was able to do something that I myself was not; because it was basically able to hold my body and my entire skin together, although it also triggered several side effects, such as a severe increase in my body weight.

The decision to take chemically produced medication was, therefore, a very costly affair for me physically, but it was only after treatment, that I was able to initiate the very radical integration of my Spiritual Energy all the way down to the cell level of my body.

My body, which of course is the dense and physical part of my energy, was simply unable to cope in the fight against my strong Spiritual Energy even though originally, the intention was for the two to work in equal cooperation. You see, the Spiritual Fire and the desire for truth were burning uncontrollably within my system, to such an extent that my body and my skin lost all its moisture. Back then I didn't understand the overall dilemma between the spiritual and the physical foundation at all in the way I understand it now. I didn't understand how fundamentally irreconcilable those two forces are, but my illness helped me to really gain clarity about the problem, so I ended up better able to accept the spirit's slow entry into the earthly physicality.

Fortunately, after a long battle, I regained my physical balance, and with the benefit of hindsight I actually find it fascinating that I became so wise regarding the very concept of Spiritual Energy through experiencing the gradual breakdown of my physical body right before my eyes. I would like to add, though, that it is now very difficult for me to recall all the physical pain that my physical breakdown entailed at the time. All I know for sure is that I have absolutely no desire to repeat the experience.

My conclusion to this course of events turned out to be the following: If I, as a spiritually conscious individual, was incapable of containing the pure Spiritual Energy within my physical body, then how could other less spiritually conscious people contain the influx of Spiritual Energy into their physical bodies?

Suddenly I understood that if Spirit in its purest form were suddenly to occupy Earth, as is the true wish of many spiritual people, the physical structure of the planet would simply collapse. All human development as well as development of all kinds of physical intelligence, knowledge and insight would therefore be completely wasted; when the Spirit burns through everything, only the essence of everything remains, which corresponds to a pure state of being, but with no physical memory on which to build human development. If this were to happen, Earth would have to start all over by developing human consciousness from scratch. Better to move ahead a bit more slowly but surely, taking both Spirit and matter into consideration at the same time and in a balanced way.

Although you are free to choose the speed of the Body Crystallization yourself, I do not recommend opening up completely to the integration of the pure spiritual consciousness in your body. I recommend that my clients, and now you as well, take one step at a time in your Crystallization Process instead and do things at a speed that you can handle. Don't look at what others do, as we all have our own individual way of integrating our spiritual consciousness into our bodies, which you will hopefully appreciate when you have read the many different Crystallization cases that I have included in 'The Crystal Human and the Crystallization Process Part I' and 'The Crystal Human and the Crystallization Process Part II'.

My sincere hope is that the two books will help you gain a better insight into your personal Crystallization Process, no matter where you are in the process, so that you may feel inspired to do things that are *right just for you*.

Kind regards,

Anni Sennov
Copenhagen, Denmark, April 2009

WHOLENESS

Please note that when I use the term 'wholeness' throughout the book, I am referring to things as a whole. 'Wholeness' means 'the whole' which originates from (w)holiness with its many different aspects of life, and allows room for everything, including our differences. The term 'wholeness' leaves plenty of space for all people so they are free to do whatever they want, and to do so in their own way – hopefully to the benefit of the 'wholeness'.

I believe that 'wholeness' is a Scandinavian phenomenon, as I often hear the word 'oneness' used in English-speaking countries. To me, 'wholeness' best describes what I refer to in this book. I sincerely hope you understand my way of expressing things.

BODY CRYSTALLIZATION

The Body Crystallization Phase

From 2009 onwards all children are born as Crystal Individuals with fully crystallized bodies that are in complete harmony with their Crystal aura structures. The children's auras, however, fluctuate in somewhat higher, i.e. faster, frequencies than their bodies, which are more physical and dense in their structure. Despite the difference in density between the aura and the body, the signalling and the force within the Crystal aura and the Crystal body are completely identical.

Although we refer to these little new Crystal Individuals as Crystal Children, who are all in full consciousness harmony with their physical body energy and their aura structure and so have an inner balance that is visibly expressed to everybody through their personalities, they are actually not yet 'fully' crystallized humans. Fully crystallized children are literally not born until 2012-13 and in the ensuing years.

In addition to focusing on the individual and their own personal balance, 'pure' Crystal Humans are extremely focused on entering into various networks in their external lives, whether in relation to their family, interests and study groups, sports teams, social groups, etc. where they function and balance in harmony with the rest of the family and the group, and where they have a mission as a whole.

As mentioned, the completely 'pure' Crystal Children, who are born with a focus on the individual and the wholeness at the same time do not begin to find their way to Earth until the period starting from 2012-13 when the focus really starts to be on holistic values in society as well. However, it is possible for all little Crystal Individuals to continue to crystallize in their relationship with the outside world during the first years of their lives. Even if this is difficult for their parents to understand, since it is difficult to envisage how small children are able to have social networks at such a young age that do not involve their parents. But indeed they can – just wait and see!

In the future, young Crystal Children will be able to recognize many faces they meet on their life journey, and they will have contact with many people on inner levels which their parents have no knowledge of and with whom the children will not connect until at a later point in their physical lives. You could say that the children have begun to prepare the social network of their earthly adult lives already at a very young age - so far, however, at a consciousness level.

From 2009-12, little Crystal Individuals are born, who are fully crystallized in their auras and bodies. These Crystal Individuals are self-contained and express a sense of balance in relation to their environment.

From 2012-13, little Crystal Children will be born, who are fully crystallized in their auras and bodies as well as in their outer network energy even though they do not have a big social network in their physical lives yet. These Crystal Children are self-contained and are also an active part of a greater, balanced Crystal Wholeness, i.e. the Crystal network.

The exact same conditions apply to adults, who are fully crystallized in their auras and bodies, as to the Crystal Children. The only real difference between Crystal Adults and Crystal Children is that Crystal Adults remember how different things were before their Crystallization. Crystal Children, on the other hand, are born with their Crystal auras and Crystal bodies as a fully integrated, cooperating and balanced energy condition right from the beginning, and cannot imagine it being any different, as this is the only energy condition they will know of in their current lives.

When adults have their Crystal aura integrated through an AuraTransformation™ today, which is only possible if they are consciously capable of fluctuating in accordance with the frequencies of the Crystal Energy, the foundation is laid for them to begin their Body Crystallization themselves – and the Body Crystallization definitely represents the most prolonged part of the Crystallization Phase.

Under normal circumstances, the body of an adult takes 3-4 years to crystallize, if the owner of the body lives a pretty balanced life. In comparison, it takes a healthy, normal, unborn Crystal Child approximately nine months to crystallize their body. A Body Crystallization that takes place during the entire pregnancy from the time of conception to birth, when the child lives under completely protected circumstances in its mother's uterus without any distracting physical external influence.

If you have taken good care of your body and your mind as an adult and if you have lived a physically healthy life, your Body Crystallization can easily start automatically, long before you decide to have your aura crystallized through an AuraTransformation™.

The same applies if you have lived close to or completely commune with nature, as nature represents the pure Spirit in physical form. Your body then follows nature's rhythm and flow, without you thinking about it, and pure, undisturbed nature is always in total harmony with the highest spiritual and physical forces at one and the same time.

By being one with nature, you allow room for the Spirit and therefore enable consciousness to fully enter your body, which is essentially what the Body Crystallization is all about. However, the Body Crystallization should not happen too quickly as the idea behind Body Crystallization is not for people to risk dying during the integration of their Spirit into their body. Many earthy-oriented people subconsciously equate 'pure spirit' with the physical death, which is why the majority of them in their body cell structure are fundamentally opposed to integrating pure Spiritual Energy into their bodies.

In the consciousness of most spiritual people, the Spirit is tantamount to pure heart energy and on the other hand represents eternal life – as humans we therefore have differing opinions of the concept of spirit, depending on our consciousness standpoint.

Anyone who has experienced being unconscious knows the feeling when the spiritual impulse enters your body with ultra short notice. The entire physical control system of the brain is turned off, so that afterwards you cannot remember what happened before you lost consciousness and passed out. The Body Crystallization Process in adults should preferably happen over a prolonged period of time for this precise reason, in order to protect the physical body from being completely overpowered by a spontaneous spiritual impulse – or death impulse if you wish – where our physical control system of the brain is completely switched off in order to make room for an externally imposed spiritual impulse.

The idea behind the Body Crystallization Process is indeed to balance Spiritual and Body Energies with each other, so that neither the Spiritual Energy nor the body has the upper hand. Most adults therefore choose to body crystallize over several years, rather than the process lasting only a short period of time. This helps avoid feeling dizzy and activation of the fainting reflex, which is otherwise only activated when the body is overloaded, for example. if you suddenly start to do physically very demanding exercises without warming up first, if you carry things that are too heavy, if you do not eat enough and/or nutrient-rich food, if you forget to drink water and if you do not get enough sleep.

The biggest advantage for people by crystallizing their auras and their bodies is that they become fully crystallized Crystal Individuals and that, in doing so, they gain their consciousness standpoint in the 9th dimension.

You see, Crystal Individuals' life mission is hidden within the cell struc-ture of their physical bodies in the 9th dimension, and this life mission is activated as the Spiritual Energy of the aura enters into their bodies and lights up each cell in the entire body, through which the cells are transformed into Crystal cells.

The Body Cell Crystallization, which is about increasing the frequency level of all the body cells and therefore becoming fully enlightened Crystal cells, significantly changes the body's energy signalling. You see, all Crystal cells grow intelligently in their own way, each with their own life mission, just as all Crystal Individuals each have their own life mission.

This now causes the meridian lines, which until now acted as optical fibre cables throughout the body each carrying their own flow of information, to no longer have the privilege of being special messengers of holistic information from the body and the Spirit and therefore the mind. All Crystal cells in the Crystal body have their own way of carrying this holistic information that originates in the body and the Spirit as a collaborating unity. This holistic information enables the Crystal cells to relate to the whole Crystal Individual, whose body they are part of, while at the same time looking after their own individual physical life mission within the body.

In the future, we are therefore going to experience many Crystal Children and Adults asking that their massage therapist and other body therapists do not massage and make contact with any areas of their bodies other than those that hurt. Crystal Individuals and Humans simply do not know how to react to stimulation given to another area than the one that hurts. They do not understand the point of stimulating another spot in the associated meridian line in order to counterbalance or move possible pain, as they do not have meridian lines like people with Soul and Indigo auras. However, Crystal Individuals and Humans still have zones on their feet, ears and hands, as well as certain areas of their bodies that relate to specific organs.

You must crystallize in your aura as well as your body in order to become a Crystal Individual with a consciousness standpoint in the 9th dimension, where your Crystal life mission is activated in your body cells.

By building up a well-developed Crystal network as a fully integrated part of your physical life, you develop from a Crystal Individual of the 9th dimension to a Crystal Human of the 13th dimension.

Case

Aura Mediator™, Anne Grethe Brandsøy, 44-year-old woman from Norway, describes her Crystallization Process as follows:

The first thing I noticed during my Crystallization was that I 'lost' my Balancing Body (author's comment: *this happens when the aura's frequency is increased from the Indigo to the Crystal level*). This probably happened during a Balancing session with Berit Reaver at the beginning of 2008. I had a somewhat peculiar feeling of being more 'free' in my body and my aura, and at the same time a feeling of being more 'whole' and balanced in my body. I sensed sort of a closeness that was connected to the aura surrounding my body. I felt even more protected than when I had the Balancing Body.

I then realized that I was no longer taking in as much of others' energy and that I was able to now be even more in my own energy without being affected by those around me. I used to walk on the street and very quickly sense the energies of the people who were passing by, but I am now completely unaffected when walking amongst large crowds... to a certain degree, of course. I can still sense the energies around me, if I use my antennae.

When I treat others, either through massage or through an AuraTransformation™, I feel the energy working inside my body. I'm not sure if this has intensified during the Crystallization – perhaps it is a gradual development.

I feel that I have become better at keeping my body in shape, and even realize a bigger need to do so. I am also better at sensing whether certain foods are good for me or not, or if they taste bad. I have an even greater need for eating healthily and enjoy taking dietary supplements. I used to be against taking them and used to forget to take them.
Generally, I also feel stronger in my body and have greater stamina than I used to. I became physically stronger right after my AuraTransformation™

but feel that I have become even stronger now and can work longer, e.g. massage, without becoming especially tired.

Physically, I have literally dropped things from my hands during brief periods of time... it was exactly as if my hands simply let go by themselves or were very weak... and come to think of it, this happened at times when I was very busy. So, when my voice used to weaken or my body used to feel tired, my body now gives me different signals, such as dropping things from my hands. This happened at the end of 2008 and I have spoken to several others who experienced it during the same period of time. I have now had some rest and no longer experience it.

Over Christmas, the flu raged in my neighbourhood and my family, and for a long time I was able to avoid catching it … however, I was the last one to get it, but a very light version that only lasted a few days.

As for the relationship to my environment, my child and my partner, I don't feel a big difference. However, I have great telepathic contact with my partner, which I have had ever since we met in March 2008. The telepathy has been at a physical as well as a mental level. In that context, I would like to share something rather unusual that happened: My partner had not undergone an AuraTransformation™ when I met him and hadn't worked with himself for very long. However, he was open to new things and ideas and quite 'willing to learn'. He doesn't like to jump into things and wanted to be sure before undergoing his AuraTransformation™ and it took a while before he got it. Before he underwent his AuraTransformation™, I couldn't sleep in the same bed as him and I had to lie down in a different room after counting sheep for a while. Since he underwent his AuraTransformation™ I have slept like a rock next to him. Our relationship has also improved and it is easier for us to know whether we will make a good couple in the long run.

As for topics that have come up, my professional life and my involvement in 'Alternativt Forum' (Alternative Forum) that organizes lectures and seminars in Florø (Norway) have taken up most of my life lately. There are so many projects and opportunities coming up at the same time... and I have always had a tendency to spread myself a bit too thin – and then nothing comes of anything. I am now more aware of this and consciously try to pinpoint the things that are most important to me. In a way I am forced to do this as I am now living more in the moment and can only do one thing at a time, which is why other projects are somehow 'forgotten'.

I have not made any big decisions during this phase, but am taking things as they come.

My mood has been good and stable during this period of time. I feel that I have a great inner calm and am optimistic about the future (PS - once in a while I have become quite upset when things were going too 'slowly', in other words, I have been somewhat impatient, and didn't want to be hindered by any unnecessary trivialities).

Things are flowing great and I even feel that I'm stressing less than I used to. I feel that the Christmas preparation went very well this year – I have never been as calm as I was this year – no stress regarding gifts or any preparation!

I am still trying to find some good, relaxing ways to exercise, also with respect to my clients who are stiff and sore, especially in the areas around their neck and back. I have tried a little Qigong. These exercises are easy to do and are supposed to increase the circulation of Chi in the body. However, since I have undergone an AuraTransformation™, I don't feel I need the spiritual thoughts that are part of the exercises, as I am already in great touch with my Chi, and also apply other methods to bring back any 'lost' Spiritual Energy.

Also regarding other treatment methods to influence the energy in my body, I have a somewhat 'mixed' experience, as I feel that these are aimed at the 'old' frequencies and thus 'draw me down'. I feel that my mood gets a bit 'flat' and I get somewhat depressed. (I sometimes also experience this if I drink alcohol). During healing and colour therapy I have experienced it as being very uncomfortable and draining (mind you, with a healer who didn't have 'the New Time Energy').

The path to a quicker Body Crystallization

With the entry of the Crystal Energy, the majority of adults and adolescents will, figuratively speaking, have an opportunity to be reborn. Not only at consciousness level as many experienced with the Indigo Energy, but also at physical level.

This is because the Spirit, which represents pure life and light, completely adopts the far denser human body, thus causing an increase in the body's frequency level.

However, it can be extremely hard on the body to be taken over by the Spirit and in addition, it takes a very long time to fully crystallize the body because the frequency of each little cell throughout the physical organism must be increased, without losing the overall balance in the process.

Since I have experienced through my own body just how big of a consciousness strain it can be for the physical organism to be subject to Body Crystallization, I have been looking for body and health products for several years that might help speed up and/or help the Body Crystallization Process in order to minimize any imbalances.

The vitamins and health products I have discovered are all characterized by a firm structure that the physical organism feels secure with and responds positively to during the prolonged restructuring phase that the Body Crystallization entails.

It usually takes quite strong vitamins to help the body through the days of particularly strong Crystallization at cell level. In addition, there is often a great need for cleansing old body slag and for strengthening the body's immune system, which is why the amount of health tablets and capsules can look pretty overwhelming on your vitamin shelf during the Crystallization Phase.

Consumption of the selected products is primarily based on intuition, as no two days are perceived alike in connection with people's Body Crystallization. It is therefore of great advantage to have several products ready on your vitamin shelf for potential use today and/or in a month and then perhaps not again for another six months.

Once the need for vitamins and dietary supplements occurs and the products are not at hand, the acute state of deficiency often leads to periodically confusing conditions within the body, and often in your mind as well. These symptoms will quickly dissipate or completely disappear, the minute you take the much-needed vitamins and herbs.

One small imbalance will not break the crystallized individual, but quite often even the feeling of a small imbalance can take up disproportionate room in people's consciousness during their Body Crystallization as they are constantly focused on their health and balance in all contexts. During the Crystallization Phase it is therefore comforting for people if the required health products are within reach at any time to balance their system. Once the products are no longer needed, you may wish to give them to someone else who needs them at the time.

Naturally, in addition to a healthy diet consisting of varied and preferably biodynamic/organic foods, plenty of vitalized water (which I am a big fan of) as well as various vitamins and health products, exercise and sex definitely contribute to a much faster and more balanced Body Crystallization. In addition, it pays to consult your reflexologist, physio and massage therapists or other kinds of body therapists regularly in order to help the body balance, stretch and better relax.

For those who do not feel great during the winter months due to the partially absent daylight, I recommend using daylight light bulbs to increase your body's vitality. The pineal gland reacts particularly well to daylight and inhibits the production of Melatonin, which normally promotes sleep. This will help you stay awake and keep you going.

Case

Aura Mediator™ Bina Miriam Christensen, 40-year-old woman from Denmark, talks about her Crystallization Process as follows:

When my Crystallization Process began in 2003 I thought I was out of balance and that I had ended up in a situation similar to the one before my AuraTransformation™. I felt depressed, overly sensitive and very tired, my grounding seemed shaky and I was unable to find my permanent footing. Whenever I felt that I was finally grounded on my platform, another shift happened and I would lose my footing again. Fortunately, Anni Sennov pointed out to me very early on that my Crystallization had started by itself. My consciousness had made the decision, without me being consciously aware of it. It was a big relief to know that I was now crystallizing and that this was what was causing my imbalances.

To crystallize means pulling back all our energy through our heart, all the energy that we - consciously or subconsciously - have placed in several places and that we now need to get back. At the same time, our energy must now be integrated into our system, right down to our cell structure, so I had indeed begun a very long and transforming process.

During the Crystallization, we as humans must learn to relate to energies in a new way - and ethics, truth, responsibility and development are expected to be some of the code words and etiquettes in the New Time Crystal Energy. The Earth ascends, as does the Indigo Human. This is why we need to cleanse our lower energies in order to become enlightened by our spirit.

Generally, I'm experiencing the Crystallization Process in waves. It is like hiking up a mountain, at times it is challenging to climb, but somewhere ahead there is a place that has been cleared for me to rest and enjoy the view after all. At other times, I spend a lot of energy hiking to finally reach a spot to rest.

The first part of my Crystallization was the worst, as my body needed to familiarize itself with the new, lighter energies that were novel to my body. I was very tired and suffered from severe headaches and felt very stressed at times. The beginning of the Crystallization is often the most difficult for many people because the body must first get to know the much faster frequencies that are now taking over the body, the mind and the senses. As my Crystallization progressed, I was able to apply my experience from the Crystallization Process in my work as an Aura Mediator™, because many of my clients had also begun to crystallize. Fortunately, I was able to help them through Balancing sessions while assuring them about the process and telling them that things were going to get easier. So, from being an individual process, I experienced that the last half of my Crystallization was an individual as well as a holistic process where I was able to help others.

As mentioned, I'm experiencing my Crystallization in waves and, depending where in the aura and the body the Crystal Energy is working on a consciousness level, some phases are more intense than others. Once I accepted this reality, which gave me a better understanding and clarity of the fact that I was becoming fused together all over again, I was able to relax more and thus make the process easier for myself.

The Crystal Energy is like a whirlwind that goes more into depth than any other energy that we've had before here on Earth, and we pull the energy into our bodies while ascending in energy. My Crystallization was intensified at times and was gentle at other times. If I had something important to do, e.g. clients coming or participating in a course, I was able to cooperate with the energy, so that it would be on stand-by for a number of days, when I needed to focus on something other than being in the Crystallization Process.

The fact that, fortunately, after my AuraTransformation™, I now had a new, stronger aura, made me feel more protected from the outside world, but there were still times when the Crystallization worked very intensely in my heart. At those times, I became very depressed and hypersensitive and cried a lot. All the sorrow I had had in life and in former incarnations, surfaced and were released. I was surprised that I carried so much sorrow because, just before my Crystallization, I didn't realize that my sorrow was as deep and as big as it was. At the same time, I was also met with quite a bit of resistance, as many external energies on Earth are not interested in spiritual development and whenever they have a chance of halting the development, it can easily happen during the Crystallization Process when we are very open and sensitive. Most people will come across this when they begin to pull their own force and power back to themselves. I often experienced that people were trying to obstruct my ideas and my projects, I was even met with strong resistance at times and had to use inner strength I had not suspected, in order to keep a cool head.

It helped to receive Balancing sessions and mild body treatments, such as reflexology and Craniosacral therapy as well as taking lots of vitamins and minerals; because the body integrates the Crystal Energy right down to cell level and thus enlightens all our cells. This process takes time and the body needs good nourishment to withstand it. We therefore need to adjust our eating habits and our vitamin and mineral supplements, simply because we move and live within a different, higher frequency and thus our body metabolizes differently. Whenever I felt stressed and anxious it was because my old body memories, which were stored deeply within my body, reminded me that it was time to cleanse out the system even more. At the beginning of my Crystallization I didn't feel that too much was happening in that area – the cleansing felt more like a deep, bottomless well - but then suddenly I felt great release and I was able to put the past behind me and 'go with the flow'. I thought it was great to take those quantum leaps while being aware of what was going on in my body and my aura.

As the Crystallization was coming to an end, I started body treatments that were more dynamic, such as active dance and shake meditations. That form of exercise really had a positive effect on me, as I was able to shake up the last, old, undesirable energies and move them out of my system quite quickly, while at the same time receiving Balancing sessions from time to time.

Personally, I had parted company from many of my old relationships, mostly old friends from before my AuraTransformation™, as we had grown apart. I now had my own family on the agenda. Family relationships and my relationship with my siblings were totally re-evaluated and our individual energies were completely separated. I realized that, although we are related, our life philosophies are very different as are many of our fundamental energies. With regard to subtle energies at a Spiritual level, my relatives and I were so different that it often surprised me that we were actually related. I then realized - somewhat like being a teenager all over again – that I needed to become independent once again as many energies and norms around our family had to be cleaned out of my life.

In the New Time Energy nothing is cocooned and the truth about conditions related to energy, situations and people always comes out e.g. it was easier for me to sweep something under the rug in the Indigo Energy if I didn't feel like dealing with it. However, during the Crystallization Phase, these truths usually hit me like a bomb and I thought, "OK, so this is how it is", whether or not I felt like it or had the time and energy to deal with it. The Crystallization was very intense for me at times and involved many 'aha experiences', and any naive conceptions I had were viewed in a different light. I started having new contemplation regarding what I really wanted to do with my life. I was more inspired to improve myself at taking a standpoint and holding on to what I believed in, to live the way I wanted, to be more clear and direct in my way of being and interacting with others, what kind of relationship I wanted to have with certain people and what I could do myself in order to meet my own needs as much as possible.

Once fully crystallized, we can keep using the energy resources within our energy structure as a knowledge bank. Spiritually it is expected of us that we continue to develop the facets that we have as humans and that we share this knowledge with others at the same time.

Since 2005, the Earth has gone through the four elements of Fire, Water, Earth and Air, which are the elements that we must integrate in connection with our Crystallization and which we can use to support us during the process at the same time. In the 5th dimension it is the Spirit that takes over the body and since the Fire element is the Crystal Energy's transformational force, Fire is the most important factor of the energy that is felt more physically in the body during the Crystallization. This is why I often woke up in the middle of the night soaked in sweat and sensing the Crystal Energy working intensely inside my heart and in my thymus gland where our new spiritual heart point resides.

Most often, the Crystal Energy works full throttle at night, and before going to sleep we can therefore ask the energy to work on some specific imbalances or topics that need to be processed.

During the Crystallization Phase I integrated more Earth, through physical activity and Balancing sessions as well, which meant that my grounding was improved and also that I became more visible to the outside world. The year of the Earth, 2007, supported me well in this (author's comments: *In 2007 it became possible to integrate the 7th-dimension Earth element here on Earth*).

So, to crystallize also means that the essential part, which is always part of us, i.e. the spirit, is expressed through our physical body as a force that helps us live, based on who we really are and what we really believe in. My Crystallization Process has enriched my life and made room for new initiatives and ways in which I want to live. The best part of the process, however, is that the strength that I have sought all my life is now within myself; a power that I can draw upon and use. I believe that people become more and more autodidactic and creative as the Crystal Energy fully enters into our bodies, because we cannot help but realize ourselves and do what we desire to do.

Recommended body and health products

In connection with their Body Crystallization, I recommend that my readers take several selected Danish body and health products, which you can buy through my Danish website **www.annisennov.dk**, where the products are currently presented in Danish only.

However, since existing European laws within the health industry do not allow me to specify non-documented effects of various vitamins and health products on my website, the products unfortunately do not specify their effect in connection with the Body Crystallization Process.

In the cases contained in *'The Crystal Human and the Crystallization Process Part I'* and *'The Crystal Human and the Crystallization Process Part II'*, several Aura Mediators™, instructors and clients mention their personal experience with various health products. These statements are based on each individual's personal experience. You will have to create your own experience and not rely too much on other people's personal experiences in connection with your personal Crystallization Process.

Neither the manufacturers, who are not aware of the publication of these two books and the effect their products may have in relation to a Body Crystallization, nor I or Good Adventures Publishing can be held responsible for the effect the mentioned products have in relation to your individual Crystallization Process.

Your personal Body Crystallization Process is your very own individual process which only you are in charge of and responsible for which, at the same time, should not keep you from taking good advice from others. For, who knows, perhaps a particular piece of advice may help you.

General products that may be of benefit to anyone in connection with their Body Crystallization Process:

- **Vitamins and minerals**

  It has always been better for me, personally, to take various vitamins and minerals as long-acting tablets that are released in the intestines over the course of 12 hours. This ensures a better absorption of the respective vitamins and minerals.

- **Herbs and root vegetables**

  It is beneficial to eat any herb and root vegetables in connection with your Body Crystallization Process, preferably a large variety at the same time.

  I did not know the advantage of eating large amounts of herbs and root vegetables myself during the first part of my Body Crystallization Phase. However, the herbs and root vegetables help your body to better relate to letting various light impulses into the cells, without affecting the overall body balance too much.

  All spiritual and light impulses of the purest kind are often very unstructured by nature, whereas the physically dense body cells are much more structured and can easily adapt to the overall physical unity that the body is. Most spiritual and light impulses that make their way into the body through the Body Crystallization are therefore comparable to cancer cells. They have a constant and persistent need for doing things their own way without really considering how the body originally functions. The physical body cells therefore perceive the penetrating spiritual impulses as disease-promoting impulses that cause physical death in small doses, which is why the immune system decides to kick in the very minute the first spiritual impulses make their way into the body.

In my experience, large amounts of herbs and root vegetables help the body feel balanced and stimulated during
the Crystallization Phase as it somehow recognizes the
energy and feels safe with it. The Body Crystallization can
therefore occur behind the scenes and within the body,
without causing unnecessary disruption when the externally imposed light impulses gradually take over the body
on par with the physical energy structure of the body's
cells. A spiritual-physical cooperation can therefore be
initiated, without the necessity for big sword fights in the
body, which can often result in severe and inexplicable
pain impulses.

- **Your body tissue needs help to achieve more calm, relaxation and greater flexibility**

  It is definitely recommended to take body and health
  products that promote calm and relaxation, as well as
  increased resilience and flexibility, during the Body Crystallization Phase when all body tissue and cells in your
  muscles and tendons are transformed from 'normal' cells
  to Crystal cells.

The cell enlightenment can be compared to a person who,
really lacking sleep, is forced to open their eyes in the
middle of the night to have a 200W light bulb shoved in
their face. This can cause the brain to completely lose its
orientation. You see, light is made up of particles that are
constantly moving, which is definitely not what the brain
needs when the person is most tired. Instead, the person
needs rest and darkness, which in this connection leads
to added peace.

The person will thus experience a stinging in their eyes,
headache and body aches from all the light that they sud-

denly have to integrate at a time when he or she is not prepared for this at all. This is exactly how the physical body often feels during the Body Crystallization Process, when it is most intense. Even if our intelligence knows what is going on, the body reacts with stress and tension every time and this often results in physical pain.

Acid cleansing:

- **Acid cleansing diets**

    For someone like me, who has been extremely affected by eczema, an acid cleansing diet is a must for your physical and personal well-being. Since the products that are 'in' very much depend on the country in which you live, I shall refrain from recommending any specific products here.

    For me, countless acid cleansings drained my body of large amounts of acid, which significantly relieved the itching, and the irritation of my skin.

- **Try to avoid garlic**

    Although this may sound strange to many people, I disco-vered the importance of avoiding garlic towards the end of my Body Crystallization Phase as well as during the time that followed, when my body had fallen completely into place and garlic simply irritated my 'clean' intestines.

Case

Aura Mediator™ Sanne Philipson, 32-year-old woman from Denmark, made the following comments on her Crystallization Phase:

I am now almost through my Body Crystallization Phase. My four elements of Fire, Water, Earth and Air are now flowing and balanced and I have never felt better. Things are flowing/happening for me like never before. It wasn't an easy journey, but it was worth it all!!

Prior to my AuraTransformation™ I was pure masculine energy and had broken pretty much every bone in my body as part of trying to put a stop to the breakdowns, traumas and abuse I had been through. None of it happened intentionally, but because I am now an Aura Mediator™, I now know that that is how it was. I have been close to death several times and in connection with my last accident, after which I was wheelchair-bound for a while, I carried out a review of my entire life. I didn't know what to do or how to begin a more balanced life, in harmony with and focused on the feminine, but I knew that that was where I wanted to go.

In the summer of 2005 I met a woman at a presentation. She told me that she was an Aura Mediator™ and funnily enough I had recently come across the phenomenon AuraTransformation™ a couple of times. I immediately knew that this was what I needed. A new aura!! The very same woman, Lisabeth Norvig, performed my AuraTransformation™ and, oh my God, was it ever the best thing that could have happened to me! I knew it the moment I left the session. I saw a different, more feminine glow in my eyes and sensed that I didn't scare away people with my presence and the things I said. I became better at putting my foot down and at feeling myself. And for the first time in my life I only felt myself, rather than everybody around me.

All my life I have had clairvoyant abilities and have always felt everything and everybody around me.

It was a whole new beginning! I quit working for the National Defence, stopped boxing and riding motorcycles; I didn't feel like being a boy anymore and began training to become an alternative therapist. My focus was redirected towards the more feminine, soft values and I realized very quickly that I was going to be an Aura Mediator™ and that was what I wanted to work towards.

In 2005 I cut all ties with my family as I felt that they were not good for me and never before had I sensed such inner peace. It is nearly impossible to break with your social heritage or to fight your own demons, when a family with the exact same issues are breathing down your neck.

In February 2007 I became a certified Aura Mediator™ through Aura Mediator Instructor™ Sofia Liv Ebling. AuraTransformation™ is the most wonderful tool for helping clients. With this tool and my intuitive abilities, which enables me to look into my clients' subconscious and feel all their baggage, physical and emotional, I am able to remove anger, sorrow, fear, eating disorders, jealousy, self-consciousness, the fear of life/death and so much more, if the client is ready for it. I cannot describe the sense of joy I feel inside when my clients get up from the couch with a different strength and clearer glow in their eyes than when they lay down on the therapist's couch. ☺

As several of my aura-transformed clients have said to me and with which I totally agree: "*An AuraTransformation™ is like coming back home to yourself*", and I would like to add "*without the old baggage*".

Due to my pre-existing injuries, my own Crystallization Process has been somewhat tougher than for most aura-transformed people. As an Aura Mediator™ my experience tells me that the Spirit cannot make its entry down to cell level until we have worked on the old trash we bring along in our baggage - because it is one thing what we remember mentally, but another that lies in our cell memory. Throughout my Crystallization Phase I have often received body therapy treatments, which I now offer myself, and Craniosacral therapy and Balancing sessions in order to facilitate the entire process and the physical cleansing.

I also quickly realized that although I have a lifestyle as healthy as I do, my body needs additional supplements, such as dietary supplements, vitamins and minerals, due to the Body Crystallization Process. I have lived very purely for several years – primarily fruit, greens and some wholegrain rye bread and have avoided all processed foods. I used to eat a lot of meat but, as my Crystallization Phase has progressed, I have wanted less and less meat and now only eat it about once a week. Instead, I am taking the dietary supplement Total Amino from BiOrto because it is important to get the eight essential amino acids that are difficult to get through a vegetarian diet alone.

The vitamin and mineral product that my body found it easiest to absorb was Vitamun. I have also loosely supplemented with e.g. Zinc to ease the absorption of my diet, B-complex to help me when I felt an 'increase or a decrease in energy', especially when I have performed AuraTransformation™ as well as in consideration of my mood, blood, hormonal system, metabolism, etc. In addition, I have been taking Silicon for my skin, hair and nails, selenium that is rich in antioxidants and also good for the immune system, cell salts from New Era, which in my experience are the easiest to absorb. Once in a while I have supplemented with vitamins A, D and E as well as iron and Vitamun. However, I do not recommend taking dietary supplements only for your well-being, but rather speak to an aura-transformed dietician, Kinesiologist, dietary advisor, etc. for optimal advice, or to do like I did. I received frequency treatments and a variety of analyses through Radionics (author's comment': *the utilization of an unusual energy or energies to produce a natural phenomenon or effects*).

In the evening I took Symbioflor for my intestinal flora, Kelpasan (iodine and seaweed) for my metabolism, EPA-GLA+ and at times two tablespoons of Udo's Choice and Pure Balance (oils with Omega 3, 6 and 9) for the elasticity and flexibility of the skin, for the joints and digestion as well as to improve my metabolism.

At bedtime I took calcium with vitamin D, which, if you take it in conjunction with magnesium and vitamin C, gives you a good night's sleep.

I have had great experience taking devil's claw when I have had strong pain, but have also taken it before bedtime for about a year - for my digestion as well as to promote the emptying function.

Walks, runs and spending time in nature have also benefited my Crystallization Process. It was good for me to feel how the water cleansed physically and mentally, provided me with mental peace and how the forest healed and grounded me. I would often sit for an hour by the water, depending on the temperature.

And, when things were at their worst, I prayed 'upwards' for things to slow down, which helped a great deal! ☺

Why Body Crystallization?

Many spiritual people wonder why it has to be so physically painful and take so long to body crystallize and why it cannot just happen overnight. The simple reason is that the purpose of the Spirit with its high-frequency (and therefore quick, sharp, truth-seeking and to many people invisible energy) is to penetrate the densest and most physical part of us, i.e. our body. If the Spiritual Energy is not integrated in small doses at a time, the body risks overreacting many times by putting the immune system on high alert which is not good for the body.

If spiritual people did not have to go through the physical part of the Crystallization Process and feel in their bodies how difficult it is to integrate a foreign energy (which the Spiritual Energy really is in relation to the body), they would be guaranteed to never understand the force, strength, intensity and persistence as well as the physically oriented solidarity connected to physical and material energy on this planet. You can thus conclude that the Body Crystallization Process helps spiritual people get to know the earthy physicality from the inside out and it is definitely a very different experience when you stand in the middle of the earthy physical condition rather than viewing it from the outside.

By being aware of the slower and more physically inter-connected structures from within, most spiritual people become much more patient towards their more physically oriented fellow humans, particularly in respect of the long processing time they choose to live with in their lives from time to time. Indeed, physically oriented people will normally have no problem living with unsatisfactory conditions at home and at work for many years without taking any action to address it. By contrast, however, spiritual people cannot understand why they simply do not change the conditions the very minute they are dissatisfied. This very simply illustrates the big difference between spiritual and physically oriented people.

Physically oriented people know everything that is needed to live life in the physical universe and how to actively engage their physical bodies and their psyche in that process. Most physically oriented people are therefore relatively cognisant about their own physical and psychological capacity regarding their personal endurance and how much strength they have. They therefore do not get stressed easily in life, not even during times of imbalance at home or at work. Instead, they stay psychologically on top by looking forward to their next vacation under sunny skies.

If their physical boundaries are compromised, however, and they are not able to do anything about it, their Spirit suddenly has free access to their body in the form of a psychological imbalance or physical illness. This can precipitate a change in their tune, since physically oriented people do not know how to relate to the Spirit when, 'without notice', it knocks on the door to all their body cells and tries to influence them towards development on a Spiritual level. They cannot relate to the Spiritual Energy because they can neither see, hear, smell, taste - nor feel it. The Spiritual Energy is therefore subconsciously perceived as an invisible enemy, with some hidden agenda penetrating their aura and physical body, because "what business does the Spiritual Energy have in there anyway"?

In order to ease the Crystallization Process, the Spiritual Energy often chooses to express itself through a variety of illnesses when it tries to get access to physically oriented people's body in an attempt to consciously upgrade their body energy. Illness directly represents a more reliable and recognizable form for the human, physically structured brain than if the Spiritual Energy chose to appear as many unstructured thoughts and feelings. The brain would then potentially freak out, with possible undesirable outcomes in the form of e.g. medication (sedatives) or admission to the psychiatric ward.

Extremely physically oriented people, with a left-brain hemisphere bias, can only relate to specific knowledge that involves measurable energy. Extremely spiritual people, with a focus on their creative right brain hemisphere, can mainly relate to non-measurable and non-structured energy. Of course, there are many people here on Earth who are in touch with both halves of their brain, but not always in a balanced way that enables them to optimally use both halves of their brain in unison. One half often predominates.

In the Indigo phase the overall consciousness development was very focused on integrating differences as masculine and feminine, spiritual and physical, light and dark as well as black and white, but not always in the same spheres. For example the Spirit of the Indigo aura is in the aura while the physicality is within the body. Both are therefore present in the individual, without being in direct touch with each other, which is why they do not have to be activated simultaneously. Similarly, this applies to the two halves of the brain of people with Indigo Energy. Both halves of the brain are activated, but not always in use at the same time.

The purpose of the Crystallization Process is to simultaneously activate both halves of the brain in people with Crystal Energy, and in doing so make room for physical and material survival systems as well as spiritually conscious processes to function side by side.

Fully crystallized Crystal Humans can thus not be defined as either spiritual or physical beings. They are characterized as expressing both a spiritual and a physical nature in a holistic, balanced and individual way that does not distinguish between masculine and feminine energies, or between light and dark, etc. The objective of the Crystallization Phase is thus to create whole, balanced Crystal Individuals who later on develop into Crystal Humans containing no opposites and where all aspects of their nature support each other in one personal expression.

Case

Aura Mediator™ and holistic therapist, Kristin Cecilie Meyer-Skottun, 34-year-old woman from Norway, talks about her Crystallization experience here:

I underwent my AuraTransformation™ as a gift from my mother who felt that any treasure she had discovered on *her* journey in her newly adopted alternative life would be a treasure for me as well. However, this gift of a treatment turned out to be very different for me and for the first time ever, I *didn't* feel any resistance. Instinctively I thought that this was great, without having the slightest idea what it was all about or the process that would follow. I received the treatment on a hotel couch in the year 2001 and the transformation took about 1.5 hours (author's comment: *the stated duration does not include a Balancing session*). I don't recall any details other than that I was told that I had Neptune and Venus Energies, without me knowing offhand what this entailed. My onward journey had really begun...

When I exited the Oslo Plaza after my transformation, rather than a dominating sense of loneliness, I had a strong feeling of being in 'safe hands' and 'connected' to something bigger. I just knew that everything that hadn't been quite in place in my life up until now would from now on fall into place for me without having the answer as to how and when. It took some time for me physically and mentally to change 26 years of thought and action patterns that had previously been based on principles about always saying 'yes' because then others would think of you as helpful – just like Florence Nightingale. Today we call it the 'good-girl syndrome'.

After the AuraTransformation™ I developed a rapidly bleeding ulcer, most likely because of my discord between my newly acquired knowledge and the changes I felt I 'ought to make' and what I actually physically manifested of this knowledge. I was quickly put on sick leave from my job as an estate and liability agent and after one year I re-educated myself under rehabilitation. I saw a Kinesiologist once a week in the following 2-3 years in order to get some help in 'landing' all the new perspectives of life and conditions that I felt the New Time Energies were forcing me to let in. I also sought out a homeopath, a Gestalt therapist, an acupuncturist and a reflexologist to get help in creating a more unstrained balance during the transition. I felt that I had to turn every stone and I had to analyze my life in detail and the way it had been up until now. Once and for all 'things' had to be put where they truly belonged. I simply felt the need to define myself inside out and to no longer let my happiness depend on how other people saw me. I decided to work independently and to help others with their personal physical and psychological development. My own process continued parallel to my clients' development and not a single day in the clinic went by without getting an 'answer' or having 'aha' experiences for myself as well. I felt a great sense of gratitude and that spiritually I had really opened up a treasure box and a new mental life, just a couple of years after the session at the Plaza.

Then suddenly out of the blue, I was covered in eczema from head to toe. Eczema was nothing new to me, as I had been plagued by it from the age of about one year old until I was 25, when I learned that the illness had developed from a physical allergy to being psychologically determined. I then realized that I needed to start using the word 'no' on par with 'yes' without feeling bad about it. That helped get rid of the eczema back then. However, the eczema, and the physical experience that followed, was like a nightmare brought back to life. My family and I had spent many years and large amounts of money on finding a lasting solution to the 'handicap', and now it was back with a vengeance. What was happening? No specialists were able to help, other than with strong ointments, and no professional wanted to acknowledge the correlation between stress, readjustment of my lifestyle and the eczema outbreak. I was crushed and desperate for an answer. Fortunately for me, I had a lot of experience in living according to the principle of 'beauty comes from within', but I still isolated myself quite a bit. At times I was very anxious and didn't want to answer the phone, unless I knew exactly who it was and what it was about, as any requests or questions that I had to decide on offhand would throw me even more off balance. I was torn between going back to the 'good-girl' image and the new self-loving and independent Kristin Cecilie.

I was emotionally torn about this for several months. I grieved, as I had had a taste of what my life could have been like from now on, as an independent businesswoman - full of energy. I didn't understand why the Universe had to stop me from genuinely helping others in the way that my Dharma/life mission had shown me.

In the midst of all the chaos, I discovered one of my now most important key *affirmations* ever, which I immediately began to work on integrating as a *more constructive truth to live by.*

An affirmation is the content of a sentence that you use to replace unproductive thoughts by repeating it several times a day until that becomes the new 'truth' and the foundation for further more productive emotions and actions. Today I still have the affirmation written down in my appointment book so that I can continue to remind myself of the most important rule in life. *"It doesn't matter what others say or do, what is most important is how I CHOOSE to relate to what others say and do and what I CHOOSE to believe about myself!"* It was hidden deeply inside of me, but it was my 'way' out of the eczema nightmare the second time around. It took a couple of years for it to be integrated at all levels and in all contexts without feeling bad at the same time. I still have setbacks in some areas whenever I wander too far from this philosophy. I now view this as a blessing - as a compass that shows me where I'm at, at any time in relation to my goal. I believe that many physical torments are merely symptoms at the beginning. Most often they will not manifest themselves if we 'listen' to what our body is trying to tell us on a number of different levels. Louise Hay's books have been very helpful to me in this area.

Towards the end of the second bout of eczema, I gradually experienced even more physical change. I started to miss my period, although I had quit smoking and using birth control in order to cleanse my body of stimuli. I experienced a different pain in my abdomen/stomach and put on weight slowly, but surely, despite an active lifestyle. After being somewhat lost in the dark for about a year, it turned out that I had developed PCOS (polycystic ovary syndrome), which, among other things, entailed multiple cysts on both my ovaries, an increase in body weight, severe menstrual pain, pimples, infertility, hormonal change and unwanted hair. The specialists I consulted explained to me that PCOS was something that I was generically predisposed for, but that it develops gradually over time in women who for different reasons experience prolonged stress and little sleep. This was a good description of my life before the AuraTransformation™. Two jobs, shift work, studies and never a 'no' to people if they asked me for something. That is how my everyday life had been ever since I finished high school and moved away from home.

As mentioned, my metabolism had changed and in the following five years I developed a chronic eye infection, I put on 25 kilos, had joint and muscle pain, cardiac valve problems, the shape of my face and my voice changed. I was constantly tired and exhausted, suffered from memory loss and lacked words whenever I wanted to say something. My nails and my hair became dry, I had irregular menstrual cycles, and my life was marked by feeling down and having a sore body. I recognized myself less and less and there was not much the doctors could do, as my blood tests were often too good to determine any medical treatment or form the basis of a clear diagnosis. I only responded very little to the medicine I received in the end.

All along I still 'knew' inside that the key to helping myself was through new, healthier thoughts and attitudes and that this would all go away by itself when the 'timing' was right, which is not always when we think it ought to happen ourselves. *Patience and timing for progress, conscious change at various levels and faith in the processes and the Universe* were my lessons during those years. I am still working on this.

I often frustrated my family along the way because they watched me fight, but also saw that I was not as desperate for 'quick-fix' solutions and medication as they were - because my gut feeling told me that medication was not the solution. Instead, I chose to live as well as I possibly could during those years in parallel with the 'symptoms' of low metabolism, and I asked the Universe to guide me in the best way possible as to what to do healthwise and when, in relation to my situation to address my health concerns related to my situation. I chose to work from then on, more consciously on changing my mindset, environment and motivation in respect of my daily choices and actions. I mainly did this through affirmation work and external consultation.

Today my best friend, Spirit mate and now also my husband and I are on the waiting list to adopt a child from abroad. We are focused on adding to our family and, if possible, it is going to be a little girl whom we would call Embla. I also have a handsome 13-year-old stepson, with whom I now find it easier to communicate. I enjoy the outdoors with two great, big, active dogs and live together with two wonderful cats that show me how to really enjoy a stress-free life. I now exercise and eat a balanced diet because I grant myself the best, not to be the 'nice girl' or to punish the - before long - 'fat part' of my body. My health is headed in the right direction and I have begun to respond to my physical initiatives, which is now about seven years on from the gift I received at the Plaza Hotel that autumn morning in 2001.

I now understand that it is not a matter of *what* I do that is most important for my balance, but rather *why* and *how* I do things that determine the outcome.

The Crystallization Process has subsequently given me new personal truths and experiences by which I now consciously choose to navigate my life. They simply keep me healthy and balanced, as long as I'm honest and genuine with myself. Personal truths, such as **sacrifice vs. investment**; each time I experience that my actions are perceived as a *sacrifice* rather than an *investment* I need to deselect them. It is possible that time will change my perception of what the action will cost me personally. Then I would rather test it again at a later point, integrate it and possibly reject it again. Or perhaps the realization of the difference between **moving and fleeing**; I had to stop fleeing from people, emotions and situations as I learned that your problems always move along with you. I am now more aware and present. I try to learn from the situation and I then move on when the time is right. I bring along all the wisdom I received from the situation and choose to leave the rest to the best of my ability. The proverb *"Nothing is forever, except change"* became an integrated part of me and I learned that balance is the most important focus of all. Abilities such as being humble enough to change concurrently with the development in and around me, without losing my essence, are now perceived as a strength rather than a weakness. *Flow, harmony and balance*: the art of remaining as *neutral* as possible *about the nature of things* has enabled me to consciously experience fantastic and magical moments after the AuraTransformation™, *while at the same time* enduring the uphill battle of making the Spirit and the body come together around the same principles. This worked well when everything seemed hopeless because I stopped worrying about e.g. whether blood sample results were good or bad. I just knew that they would stabilize once I had learned and integrated the essential lessons of learning to live in a more balanced way and according to the *New Time Energies*. "Life is a school of sorrow, joy, happiness and love as the main subjects" as my mother always used to say. That is indeed how the entire Crystallization Process has worked for me as well.

I am now living well with these test periods' during my Crystallization Process. I *choose* to put myself in the driver's seat of *my* life and now have the feeling of holding my happiness in *my* own hands to a greater extent. All of this and the closeness to nature give me a sense of happiness and balance no matter how things are then and there. The Crystallization Period has shown me the importance of continuously trying to live a balanced life at all levels! Thank you so much for the gift Mum!

Motivational sources

Stress, in particular, can motivate physically oriented people, whose primary focus is on the visible, physical and material factors in life, towards personal and spiritual development. Stress most often occurs when a person has no decisive influence on the course of his or her own day either on the job or at home. These stressors may come in the form of changes in working hours, external professional conditions placing the person in a poorer position; colleagues being absent indefinitely due to e.g. illness, which can lead to an increased work load for the person, or if the children or other family members are chronically ill and need care, which causes the person to miss work.

Stress may also occur when transport options are unstable and if there are changes in the person's personal life, such as a move, child birth, first day of school or daycare, divorce, etc. and last, but not least, if the children need extra supervision due to poor behaviour on a regular basis. If anything, this can be really stressful for the parents and cause them to lose perspective in many different areas of their lives, because they constantly need to be watchful of their children and cannot always relax when they need to.

There are many different stress triggers, but what they all have in common is that, for an undefined period of time, you are subject to the needs, behaviour and decisions of others. This may be okay if you have accepted this ahead of time and if you have had the time and opportunity to adapt personally and adjust your everyday life to handle the required adjustment. However, physically oriented people rarely have this opportunity when it is time for them to body crystallize.

An AuraTransformation™ can therefore end up being the solution for many physically oriented people when they choose to gather their aura and charisma in order to maintain their everyday perspective and hold themselves and their (perhaps impossible) children together, even though they may find it difficult to relate to the invisible part of themselves.

Since the physical person is able to gather him or herself much better and so usually feels more like a whole person, the AuraTransformation™ helps the person to better manage their everyday lives and creates improved conditions for the Body Crystallization of the physically oriented person. In addition, the AuraTransformation™/Aura Crystallization keeps the person from feeling that death is paying a visit each time the Spirit is about to become further integrated into the body. Instead, the spirit's further integration into the body contributes to clarifying what the person really wants with his or her life and to defining their personal boundaries.

In other words, there is a positively loaded energy clarification at cell level, rather than the person seeing the Crystallization Process as a penetrating disintegration of the existing body cell structure.

If physically oriented people refrain from undergoing an AuraTransformation™ they can still easily start to body crystallize without crystallizing in their aura and charisma at the same time. This applies to all physically oriented people who lead a healthy and balanced life and get the required exercise.

However, if they do not live and eat healthily, do not get exercise and if they do not undergo an AuraTransformation™ either, illness and stress will likely present their ugly faces to provoke them into living healthier. If they subsequently change their lifestyle, their Body Crystallization can take place over several years through a healthy lifestyle, exercise, meditation, added rest, intake of dietary supplements, time spent in nature, etc.

Spiritual people, whose main focus is on humane and non-tangible, immaterial factors in life, are not always as hard hit health-wise as many physically oriented people. Instead, they risk being hit in their personal charisma and energy protection or lack thereof.

If spiritual people at Soul level suffer a great tragedy or are close to death in some other way, or if they voluntarily try to integrate the pure Spiritual Energy into their body through various forms of consciousness energy work, the Spiritual Energy will burn uncontrolled through their Soul aura and leave them without any energy protection and personal charisma and magnetism. This happens because pure Spiritual Energy corresponds to high-frequency Fire, which is able, in record time, to break down all physicality, which is exactly what the Soul Energy is made up of.

The Soul Energy is much more physically dense in its structure than the previous Spiritual Energy, and, when it comes to energy, the Soul aura is an energy structure that belongs to this planet, which has to do with the reincarnation system that all Soul people are part of.

Just like all other physical energies and structures on this Earth, the Soul Energy consists of flammable material, so that when you lose your Soul aura because the Spirit has burned it up, you lose your energy protection and magnetism at the same time as well as your personal place in the Soul reincarnation system, because you have either outgrown the system or phased out your personal karma.

It is therefore suitable to find a new consciousness platform here on Earth where the Spiritual Energy can be fully and completely integrated into the body and the aura with a view to being acted out through a more current life mission – and fortunately a Spiritual aura cannot be lost like the Soul aura.

Many spiritual people can therefore carry a totally burned out Soul aura (or none at all) around their bodies and if so desired, this aura must now be recollected in new and higher energy frequencies in the 5th dimension that match the Fire element as well as the Spiritual Energy.

Spiritual people may be affected with health issues, which at times can be quite hard, but they are first and foremost affected in their outer human boundaries and their finances. This usually occurs because, they do not fully understand or appreciate the material and human value of either until they have lost their partner, children, friends, money, home, job and prestige, etc. An AuraTransformation™ is thus often the only sustainable solution for them to collect themselves and their charisma, after which they can begin to be present in a much more human way in the earthly dimension.

Not long after their AuraTransformation™, however, their Body Crystallization will automatically begin as a direct continuation of the Aura Crystallization, which has been initiated through their AuraTransformation™. As far as I know, Body Crystallization is inevitable for all spiritual beings if they wish to live an earthly-spiritual balanced life, as it makes them land here on Earth and move into their physical bodies with their full spiritual consciousness.

Case

Vibeke Fraling, 39-year-old woman from Denmark shares her Crystallization story:

I underwent an AuraTransformation™ in March 2008, but according to my Aura Mediator™ I had already begun my Crystallization Process before then. I don't know exactly when it started as I had been working on my personal development and awakening for several years prior to the transformation. Nevertheless I'm convinced that a landmark decision in 2007 truly got it going. I was a 37-year-old single mom with two children aged ten and eight. In January 2007 I decided to work on breaking with some of the convictions that prohibited me from being in a healthy, developing relationship. I worked on this by using tools that I had from my background as a personal coach. I needed to integrate a belief in my own self-esteem in order to set a dignified standard for myself. In March I met my current boyfriend. I now feel loved and wanted for who I am, as opposed to in my previous relationships, and that security has enabled my rapid development since then.

In June 2007 I completed my studies as a teacher and during the last semester I was chronically tired, almost worn out and ready to drop from exhaustion. Lots of old discomforts briefly reappeared, such as my old pelvic joint pain from my first pregnancy in 1995, strep throat, stiff neck, headaches and irritable bowel syndrome. During this time I saw a massage therapist once a month where, in addition to the massage itself, I received feedback on my personal development and also advice on dietary supplements. At the time I was only taking ordinary vitamins and my massage therapist recommended various sugars. I also learned that I function better when I eat lots of fruit, which is why I made a fruit smoothie every morning. I realized that the sugars and the fruit reduced my craving for sweets tremendously while it helped me avoid headaches and mid-afternoon fatigue.

In 2007 I started going to the gym five days a week. It helped calm my mind and kept me from falling back into old, useless mindsets. It was only possible for me to exercise so intensely because of an examination period when I experienced a minimal need to study. I accepted the consequences, listened to my intuition and didn't study, directly contrary to what I would usually do. Instead, I merely prepared for the examination and continued to develop the model I had developed for the subject and its content. To some people this was very risky, whereas my closest girlfriends and fellow students took my decision with ease. It turned out to be the right decision. I got what corresponds to an A+.

After exams in June, my body completely gave up. I developed a fever and flu-like symptoms and suffered from this almost the entire summer. At the same time I was totally down. I was almost overly sensitive and either cried over anything, or withdrew and experienced everything from the observer's point of view. After the summer I began to study for my Master's Degree in Educational Philosophy at the Danish School of Education (Aarhus University). I found it very easy, and yet I didn't. I didn't thrive in the mental environment. The theories we studied lacked balance, i.e. I constantly felt that we were stuck in the old way of thinking and that we didn't dare or weren't allowed to think on our own. I couldn't stand the hierarchical thinking of the system of which the training and its content were made up. I felt as if we encouraged our inner experts to move outside ourselves and into others, which is a way to sustain a balance of power that is easily kept alive by fear and a feeling of inadequacy, rather than drawing the expert back into ourselves and having faith in our own intuition. This was a new feeling and experience, as I used to love studying theories as a student teacher. I chose to take a leave of absence from my studies and got a job as a teacher after the first semester.

Another big decision in 2007 was the decision to buy a house with my boyfriend. Previously, I couldn't imagine being in such large debt and generally I would start to hyperventilate at anything that had to do with finances, lie awake at night and believe that I wasn't capable of managing my own finances. I gathered the courage and worked on this. The purchase of the house turned out to be an even bigger project, as we ended up building a house ourselves. I have no idea how I found the courage and the energy to embark on this. In addition, my boyfriend and I decided to add to our family, and I got pregnant right away.

I took over a class of 16 students in January 2008. It was a class that my colleagues called 'the school's worst class' that was impossible to teach. It was never quiet for 30 seconds at a time and there was severe bullying amongst the students. Several children had ADHD or Asperger's disease and some children had other periodic learning difficulties. In addition, it was a split class of grades 4-6 within the corresponding age groups. I decided to drop traditional teaching methods for the first month to focus on establishing a class culture based on respect for each other, the differences between each of the students, as well as humour. In order to do so, I needed to let the students know and feel that I didn't view them as problem children, but rather as wonderful individuals who each had something to contribute and who each had individual needs to be seen and heard. I also had to teach them a set of social rules, such as putting up their hand and waiting for their turn to speak, as well as how to speak to, and about, each other. After two weeks it was reasonably quiet in the classroom during my classes and I was able to split the class into groups and work. After one and a half months the class was able to select their own chairperson, who understood the process of the class picking their new seats themselves. During my classes we would laugh a lot and we always had time to talk about the what, why and how in relation to topics that we were working on. I loved those kids and I think they liked me, too.

I learned to deviate from my plans and to follow my intuition instead, in relation to my students as well as professionally. My intention to establish a nice atmosphere as a prerequisite for learning worked. Whether I managed to teach the students anything educationally, I don't know, but I have no doubt that I touched them personally.

During this time I wanted to discuss the school's general educational policies as I felt they were somewhat unsuitable, and I questioned other educational matters at work, which prompted my leader to ask me to an unofficial staff development interview. After a little less than three months I was given a notice of dismissal.

In my personal life I had a big clash with my mother-in-law around the same time, which was very challenging for the relationship with my boyfriend as well. However, once again I remained calm inside and was convinced that something good would come out of it. My intuition once again proved to be correct. This disagreement led to a better relationship not only between my boyfriend and me, but also with my mother-in-law.

That is when I started to have backaches and pelvic joint pain and sought out a Craniosacral therapist, who is also an Aura Mediator™ and, as mentioned, I underwent my AuraTransformation™ in March 2008.

During what was probably the beginning of the Crystallization Phase of my body, I learned to let go of my neurotic need to follow systems and rules, and to listen to and follow my own intuition instead. I learned to state my opinion clearly and to stick to it even during headwind. I learned to say what I mean without hurting others. I found out that confrontation doesn't necessarily mean that you are disliked or that it's the end of the world. I feel that I am able to relax and just be myself and that the only thing I lost was my job. However, my intuition tells me that a better one will come along, so I remain calm.

The physical body and your health

There are countless ways of body crystallizing – some people start to crystallize in their heart and then crystallize in the rest of their body, while others crystallize in their body and then in their heart.

Some start by crystallizing in their skin while others crystallize in one organ at a time and then the surrounding muscles, tendons and tissues. Then again there are those, who crystallize sporadically throughout their body, and cannot make head or tail of things during the process. Eventually things will turn out well, though, and the entire body will definitely fully crystallize at some point. But, what does it really feel like when the body crystallizes?

It often feels as if you had been run over by a steamroller…! There is a sense of ache and pressure in those places where the body is crystallizing and at times it feels as if there is not enough room for each organ and body part in the system. You do not doubt for one minute that things are working at full speed around the cells when the Body Crystallization is working hard, because it feels as if the entire machinery is working at once.

You may experience warm, burning, stinging, ice cold, prickling and/ or tickling sensations and often the very best way to react to the entire process is to simply lie down and get some rest. This is because when the brain completely shuts off and lets the body work at its own pace without interfering in the process, the process usually runs smoothly and painlessly.

Sometimes you may hear awful sounds from your body that do not always sound human, and this is not just because you fart, burp, have the hiccups or heart burn. It might be the heart that makes a squeaking sound, which no physician can explain based on general anatomy and pathology. Even knees, elbows and necks can give off bad squeaking and creaking sounds from time to time, with no relation to old injuries, and fortunately the potential irritation only occurs in that particular part of the body for a limited time.

As soon as the body is fully crystallized in one place it continues the process somewhere else, unless you crystallize in all cells at the same time, which I have yet to hear that anyone has done. This is however, an exact worst-case scenario that you should try to avoid, so you do not go completely crazy during the process. Our physically structured brain would not be able to cope with such a situation, which would probably more likely cause physical death than a radical transformation of the entire cells in our body.

If various problems related to the body, such as pain, irritation, skin problems and high blood pressure persist for a bit too long and you do not feel safe, you should naturally contact your doctor and perhaps accept prescription medication to help regulate and/or balance possible physical imbalances.

Many spiritual people, however, find it difficult to accept it if they have to take chemically produced medicine in order to help their body function normally during the Body Crystallization Process. Physical challenges can easily happen if the frequency increases and subsequently the enlightenment of each individual body cell occurs too quickly - because then the cells cannot stay collected and they lose their original physical coding. One of the purposes of chemically produced medicine is to help a sick body that is not functioning optimally to build up or reproduce a damaged cell structure corresponding to those of a normal-functioning body. In many instances chemically produced medicine acts as a copy of selected body processes and so contains certain kinds of coding that can help activate the respective body processes to function normally. This is why chemically produced medicine can be positive in helping the cell memory on the right path if the Body Crystallization Process has happened too quickly resulting in potential memory loss at cell level.

However, it is always very important to be aware of various side effects when taking chemically produced medicine, in order that other places in the body are not harmed more than the place where the body currently needs the additional help.

Natural medicine and various dietary supplements can help a sick and weakened body gain increased strength and vitality in many ways, but it cannot recreate a completely destroyed body and cell structure.

Natural medicine cannot instruct the body on how to function at cell level either, if the cell memory has been lost. So, in order to achieve a positive, useful effect from the use of various kinds of natural medicine, there must be one or more remnants of cell memory left in the body, which the body can continue to build on, as natural medicine itself is not able to do anything about the unbalanced situation.

Natural medicine may increase vitality in all healthy heart cells, but that will not help potentially damaged liver cells if these have completely lost their cell memory. A variety of different kinds of natural medicine, together with a healthy diet and lifestyle, however, is the very best supplement to complete a relatively positive and balanced Body Crystallization Process. However, this requires that the body is capable of holding itself together during the process, as the Spirit is an undeniably tough co-player whilst integrating right down to cell level.

As it is quite difficult to touch on all body symptoms that may occur in connection with various people's Body Crystallization, I have chosen to briefly describe the most common symptoms that I have either experienced myself or heard of from someone else:

Eczema and other skin problems

Since Spiritual Energy and Spiritual Fire are identical, many people get very dry skin and eczema-like conditions when their Body Crystallization is in full progress. During the Body Crystallization the skin cells have difficulty retaining the moisture and the skin thus runs a risk of cracking or developing eczema-like spots that resemble the remains of a burn. Therefore it is important to apply a good, nourishing moisturizer daily, which can help the skin maintain its moisture balance.

I personally experienced that my skin and the underlying tissue got completely dry and I felt like I was a deeply integrated part of the Sahara desert... Although I used thick moisturizing lotions and nourishing creams 24/7, it was all absorbed in no time and the cream disappeared from the surface of my skin in a split second. If I applied nourishing oils, which many recommended that I do, it was as if my skin got even drier once the oil had been absorbed by my skin, which made my 'Sahara feeling' even worse than before.

It was as if there were no film between my outer skin and the remaining organs inside my body, so many times I really felt that if I forgot to eat, I could just get full by applying lotion, which would be absorbed into my body anyway.

When this had gone on for several months and the situation seemed like it was only going to get worse with large, open burn-like flesh wounds, I gave in to taking large amounts of cortisone in pill form, which immediately made my skin look like a perfect wax model. Those pills were simply able to do something I was incapable of doing spiritually and physically myself. You see, they were able to program my skin cells to behave in a balanced way. I could not even spot a small scratch or irregularity on my entire body, but in return I put on 20 kilos within a relatively short period of time, which I definitely do not recommend.

When I got off the cortisone pills, which I had to if I wanted to avoid ending up with the shape of a big mama, it went completely downhill again – this time with an added 20 kilos. Fortunately, after a month of hell, it was recommended to me that I apply cortisone ointment instead, and this helped in record time – exactly four days – without putting on additional weight. In return I was not allowed to be in the sun, which was no problem for me, as my nightmare was unfolding in the wintertime.

With the cortisone ointment my skin was now given a chance to rediscover its original balance while I took large amounts of vitamins, minerals and health products, all of which helped the rest of my body recover and crystallize even more. The final result was, however, that I developed an allergy to tobacco smoke, which I can easily live with, as I no longer have severe allergic reactions to anything else, and my skin is now strong and healthy again.

With my Body Crystallization Process being anything but enjoyable, I have thus experienced in my own body having to team up with a chemically produced 'support therapist', i.e. cortisone, on a daily basis, which helped my skin cells crystallize in a much more balanced way than they were capable of themselves during the Body Crystallization Process.

I have always been very outgoing by nature and in continuation of this openness I have always been very open regarding anything to do with Spiritual Energy, which I cannot recommend during the Body Crystallization Phase. You see, the Body Crystallization Phase is a balancing phase that works towards an even integration of Spirit and matter at cell level and I mistakenly thought that it was a matter of fully integrating the Spiritual Energy, regardless of the physical price.

Today I know from personal experience that integrating pure Spiritual Energy into a physical body is no laughing matter and should not be taken lightly. It is an extremely exhaustive process that can be physically painful, often in cruel and uncomfortable ways.

After experiencing the extremely tough eczema journey myself, I heard about several health products that could do wonders for skin with eczema. Personally, however, I cannot confirm or dismiss the effect of those products as I was cured by the time I learned about them.

On the other hand, I can testify that it is extremely good for the body's balance to drink plenty of vitalized water, which is water with self-cleaning abilities, where the frequency of the water is much higher than in regular drinking water or bottled spring water.

High blood pressure

If you suffer from high blood pressure, it is a sign that the Spirit has taken over your body. The Spirit is essentially trying to set the pace exactly as it wants it to be, which often leads to a pace that is much too high and, that the physically dense part of the system cannot naturally keep up with.

If you have high blood pressure it is highly recommended that you see a doctor. You may also wish to source medicines for high blood pressure consisting of herbs and health products that can support prescription medication. Remember though to keep a fine balance between taking any prescription medication and various health products to avoid the double effect with a much too sudden decrease in blood pressure as a result.

Too much acid in the body

Having too much acid in the body is by far the most pervasive problem in relation to Body Crystallization. Once the Spirit takes over the body, the amount of acid in the body also dramatically increases, as the Spiritual Energy produces acid. Therefore the need for a basic diet increases, which includes green vegetables, potatoes, root vegetables, cabbage, pumpkin, onion, lettuce, herbs, ginger, raisins, apples, pears, plums, berries, etc. In addition, I also recommend taking acid-cleansing health products on an ongoing basis.

Unfortunately, cleansing the body of acids is an ever-occurring topic during the entire Body Crystallization Phase, in order that any discomfort (such as increased blood pressure, joint and muscle pain, obesity, stress, dizziness, viruses and various inflammations in the body) is prevented.

Physical exhaustion

Physical exhaustion during the Body Crystallization Phase can be an indication that you must be careful not to exercise too much at times. The feeling of exhaustion can be a way for the body to tell you that it needs rest to cope with the amount of Spiritual Energy that is being integrated into the cell level of, for example the muscles.

The Spiritual Energy is an extremely fast energy, whereas the body structure is a slower energy. Therefore, when the muscles are forced to work extra hard during the Body Crystallization through physical training sometimes the brain mistakenly thinks that it is the Spiritual Energy that is trying to enter the muscle cells. This is why the brain raises the alarm for the entire body and tells it to relax completely. The body subsequently reacts to the signal by experiencing an acute condition of exhaustion that is supposed to make the body rest immediately in order to let the Spiritual Energy penetrate the cell structure without problem. This feeling of exhaustion, however, does not always have to do with the Body Crystallization, which is why it is important to break the immediate feeling of fatigue by being conscious about exactly what is happening in the situation.

During the Body Crystallization, the brain is often our own worst enemy, as it does not always know the difference between the old and new signalling in the body. It may therefore require external help to figure out when it is time to relax and when it is okay to keep going.

It is therefore extremely desirable for the system as a whole - for both the body and the aura - to become balanced through an Aura Mediator™ when and if the body and the mind experience brief or prolonged states of exhaustion.

A feeling of imbalance in the body

When your platform is in the process of changing (which it very much is during the Body Crystallization) it sometimes feels as if the ground is moving under your feet. In most people, this produces a feeling of imbalance and/or dizziness in the body, somewhat like when you have been at sea for several days and suddenly disembark for a couple of hours and then return to the ship. The transition from one element to another and from one platform to another can be so stressful for the brain that it stops relating to what it is dealing with. It therefore either reacts with a sensation of imbalance in the body, or pronounced dizziness.

The brain is not always aware of whether it is dealing with external physical or inner consciousness conditions. Anything it has not done before is always perceived as something completely new, and it still constantly tries to relate it to something familiar, which is completely impossible when it concerns integrating the New Time Energy.

It therefore takes a high degree of will, intelligence and consciousness insight to continuously give the brain directions as to how to understand exactly what it is dealing with when the Crystal impulses are intruding, so that it does not just react by sending off various familiar signals into the body, which in reality has nothing to do with the new condition. Quite often the brain needs guidance in how to refrain from acting, which a Balancing session by an Aura Mediator™ can help with, as well as intake of vitamins and minerals, particularly vitamin B.

Recurrence of old pain

Old physical pain can easily recurs during the Body Crystallization. Suddenly it is as if it were always looming beneath the surface and never really left the system. These old feelings that relate to a corresponding old pain can reappear, but this merely happens in order for the balance to occur deep down, so that the cell memory can let go of the old experience once and for all.

Massage therapy and other kinds of body therapy as well as Balancing sessions by an Aura Mediator™ can often help the body let go of any old cell memory in a balanced way.

Discouragement

The Body Crystallization Process can often be accompanied by long and persistent periods of hopelessness and despondency. These feelings, which are similar in many ways, appear simply because you are unable to predict the duration of the total Crystallization Process. The process may take another 100 years or you may be fully crystallized in a couple of months – but who knows for sure? Nevertheless, it often feels like there are at least 100 years to go before the Crystallization is completely in place in the body, as it is very laborious work to feel all your inner body processes on the outside.

This is why, from time to time, so many people feel very old and worn out on the inside, even though they are young of age. However, those in their environment rarely notice this, as fortunately it is a condition that can change in a split second if something exciting suddenly happens in their life.

In such instances it can be beneficial to have your energies balanced by an Aura Mediator™.

Tightness in the chest around the Thymus gland

The Thymus gland is home to the new Heart Chakra and this is where the Crystal Energy has its consciousness origin in the Crystal body. However, the Crystal cells of the entire body are equally intelligent in their own way, which is why the degree of Crystal consciousness is just as high in the liver, the feet and the rectum as in the mind and the heart.

Indeed each cell's function in the body is often very different, even though the consciousness clarity is completely identical in each and every Crystal cell throughout the human body.

When you experience tightness in the chest around the Thymus gland it is often a sign that the heart is in the process of crystallizing which can happen at any given time during the Body Crystallization Process. There is not one specific time that is best suited for Crystallization of the heart. The heart Crystallization can happen first or last, and regardless of when, it is perceived to be right in every situation.

When the heart crystallizes it feels like it is burning, stinging or pressing in the chest around the Thymus gland, which is located between the throat and the sternum.
If, however, the pressure is felt around the physical heart, which naturally needs to crystallize as well, it may be due to stress. In that case it is recommended that you see a doctor, unless you have a strong feeling that the irritation is related to your Body Crystallization.

Once the Crystallization of the Thymus gland has taken place, you will become significantly better at integrating your spiritual perspective in your physical realism as a human being.

Pain in the bone structure, joints and muscles

When it is time for the body to crystallize its bone structure, most people will experience pain all the way to the bone, which is usually quite painful and unfortunately there is not much you can do about this.

Joint and muscle pain are also some of the many little everyday 'joys' that you can experience when you are in the process of crystallizing.

My best advice is to take a daily supplement of vitamins and minerals in addition to lots of herbs and root vegetables, and perhaps health products, that can help increase the flexibility in your joints and muscles to make the pain go away by itself as quickly as possible.

Obesity

Very spiritual people sometimes tend to be obese due to a lack of physical structure in their body, where everything simply flows in and out of each other without being able to stay in shape.

Similarly, many physically oriented people tend to be obese, but in their case this is due to energy ties and/or blockages around the body. Once the Spiritual Energy finds its way into the body, it tries to force the speed of the integration to increase, and the physical part of the cell structure is not always able to keep up. The physical cell structure then tries to resist by increasing the physicality and becoming even more impenetrable for the Spiritual Energy, which often leads to an increase in body weight.

Obesity in connection with the Body Crystallization Phase is primarily due to cooperation challenges or difficulties between the Spiritual Energy and the physical cell structure.

Metabolism problems

Together with the adrenal cortex, the Thyroid is one of the most exposed places in the body during the Body Crystallization and when the Thyroid does not function properly, it leads to either a high or a low metabolism. If this condition results in physical discomfort, you should see your doctor.

In addition, it is very important to have a basic, preferably biodynamic/ organic diet, to take dietary supplements and drink plenty of vitalized water and to try to avoid low-vibration foods and drinks, such as alcohol, coffee, white sugar, pork and chemically produced foods containing e-substances, additives and preservatives.

Loss of voice

When it is time to crystallize in the neck area, specifically the vocal chords, many people lose their voice for a few days, which may happen several times over an extended period of time. Apparently the voice is one of the few physical body functions that does not know how to make a change in frequency without completely shutting down while it is going on. Those who do not experience a radical loss of voice will instead experience irritation and/or an unstable vocal pitch from time to time.

Stress

Both the body and the mind often trigger stress if you are subject to the needs, behaviour and decisions of others for an extended and indefinite period of time, when you either do not have the possibility of adjusting yourself or your everyday life to be able to handle the stress.

When the body crystallizes it is sometimes subject to a high degree of stress because the brain is not always able to cope with the current phase of the Crystallization. Therefore, the body becomes weak and you become more susceptible to illness and mental imbalance. It is therefore extremely important to give your body added support through vitamins, minerals and perhaps dietary supplements to keep any viruses from entering into your body system.

Gentle massage and other de-stressing body treatments as well as Balancing sessions by an Aura Mediator™ can often help reduce stress, but these kinds of treatments are often not enough on their own without also taking vitamins, minerals and relevant dietary supplements.

Managing the pace of the Body Crystallization

Once your Body Crystallization Process has begun, you only have limited opportunity, at certain times to influence the pace of the process yourself. It takes an extremely focused mental consciousness and/or physical stubbornness to put a lid on your physical Crystallization Process, which however can be advantageous if you have to write an exam or if you have an important job interview. It is also possible to partially control the process by taking extra amounts of vitamin B-complex, which enhances the vital functions of the brain and creates mental clarity.

Dizziness

Dizziness often occurs during the Body Crystallization Process when large amounts of Spiritual Energy try to enter the body at the same time. High blood pressure or a virus in the balance nerve can also cause this, but these reactions are often triggered by the exact same phenomenon, i.e. a large amount of Spiritual Energy that is trying to enter the body in record time.

It can be beneficial to take vitamin B that contains large amounts of the entire vitamin B-complex, supplementing with relaxing health products and perhaps a glass of red wine, such as Merlot or Shiraz, which can all help to collect the mind. Alternatively, you have to remain completely calm until the dizziness goes away by itself, which happens once the present download of Spiritual Energy has settled in the body.

Virus in the body

Inner inflammatory and viral conditions in the body are often caused by a predominance of acid in the body – for more information on this, please read page 67 - regarding *'Too much acid in the body'* – which is why it is even more necessary to cleanse the body and its organs of acid. Try to eat as healthily as possible and avoid unhealthy saturated fats, as this can contribute to a renewed outbreak of inner inflammatory conditions. Eat unsaturated fats instead, which are usually found in vegetable oils, such as olive oil, in avocados, nuts and almonds - and drink plenty of vitalized water.

Changed sleep pattern

The sleep pattern changes numerous times during the Body Crystallization as the body works at full throttle from time to time, both at spiritual and cell level at the same time. It is therefore difficult to predict during the day how much you will sleep at night.

Sometimes you have aches and pain all over and other times it only hurts in one or two places in your body. Sometimes your brain is working in overdrive and it feels like a pressure cooker that is about to explode, and you cannot relate to which body parts need to go through the machinery. Other times your brain feels as if it is out of order. At times it is like a light is on inside your mind all night, which leads to a bad night's sleep, and other times your entire system says goodnight and completely closes down as soon as your head touches the pillow.

Depending on where you are at in your Body Crystallization Process and which parts of your body are in the process of crystallizing, your body will respond accordingly, without your brain being able to pre-adjust itself to the current situation. This is why your sleep and your need for sleep can be similarly difficult to regulate.

Case

Aura Mediator™ Ingar Pedersen, who is 38 years old and from Northern Norway, talks about his personal transformation process where the Body Crystallization Process did not impact his life in an inconvenient way, as his connection to Northern Norwegian nature had already completed much of the Body Crystallization work for him during his childhood:

I underwent my AuraTransformation™ in June 2007. During the session itself I clearly felt the energies in my body and in a way it felt like small electric impulses going through my body. At times I got dizzy and light-headed.

Right after the session I felt a bit tired and my body felt heavy - most of all I felt like lying down and going to sleep. Over the next three days I was very sensitive to being close to people - it sort of felt like people were getting too close to me physically. However, this feeling disappeared after my energies settled and balanced throughout my body.

After my transformation I have become increasingly conscious about what feels right or wrong for me, what feels wrong to do or be part of, as if I am now in better touch with my own intuition and my inner truth. If for example I sit together with some people I know, and they start talking about someone else behind their back in a negative way, I immediately don't feel well and want to leave, which is something I do every so often as it doesn't feel good to listen to the negative talk.

I have also become more aware of following my own needs and wants and at listening to my intuition and my heart. This applies to anything I encounter in my everyday life. I also quickly sense if people around me are negative or angry, I often try to avoid spending time with them as I pick up on this so easily and I don't like the feeling. I also feel that I am now much calmer and more centered, which is reflected in the fact that I don't get carried away in the daily dramas that often arise from little things.

Physically I haven't felt much, other than the fact that it is easier for me to sense energies in and around me. At the beginning after my AuraTransformation™ I did balancing exercises almost every night before lying down to center and balance my energies. I have always been fond of sports and exercise, I have been physically active my entire life, which means that I'm in great shape. I believe that this has facilitated the Crystallization and the energy work in my body and my mind.

Regarding my diet I have been focused on eating healthily for several years, but have probably become even more focused on what I eat and drink after the transformation. I am not particularly fond of heavy meat dishes and my alcohol consumption is very limited, once in a while I'll have a couple of beers or a glass of wine with a good meal.

I am not sure if my personal charisma has changed much after the transformation, I haven't had much feedback from my family and friends regarding my personality and my charisma. I was living on my own after the transformation so no one was able to follow my development closely. However, I have probably become more tolerant and balanced in relation to what others say and do.

I grew up in Northern Norway and still live there. This has probably affected both my Body Crystallization and me. In Northern Norway the conditions are often pretty rough, and this is why we are forced to live with a high degree of respect for the forces of nature including the weather conditions.
I enjoy being in nature and this has probably been reinforced after the transformation.
I spend a lot of time outside in bad weather because of my job and the weather has always been a factor that I have had to take into consideration. Although, the climate is tough, I wouldn't say that I experience this as a negative as, in a sense, you really feel that you are alive when the weather is so extreme and you become more aware of how your body is feeling.

General conditions during and after the Body Crystallization

I have chosen to include some general information on conditions or challenges – however you choose to view it - that are relevant for most people in connection with their Body Crystallization Process and for the majority of the fully crystallized Crystal Humans:

Asthma-like conditions as a reaction to tobacco smoke

Many Crystal Children have a low tolerance for tobacco smoke and they tend to develop asthma and allergies if they are exposed to large amounts of tobacco smoke, e.g. at home.

The same applies to many adults during or after their Crystallization Process when they may suddenly experience an allergic reaction to smoke particles, although these have never bothered them before. For that reason many adults stop smoking, either during or after their Body Crystallization Process, as tobacco smoke suddenly starts to bother them.

Body treatments and energy balancing

During their Body Crystallization, many people choose to balance the spirit's journey into the body through Reiki healing and Craniosacral therapy, etc., both of which open up the energy flow in the body, and which mostly works very well at the beginning of the Body Crystallization Process. However, several people have told me that those kinds of treatments were not able to help them when they were further along in their Body Crystallization Process, while a few people have expressed the opposite, so this must be assessed individually. I personally have no experience with either form of treatment in relation to Body Crystallization.

As the Body Crystallization completely changes the frequency structure and thus the degree of enlightenment in each cell, the body's energy signalling processes change accordingly

in quite a dramatic way. This means that all Crystal cells in the body become intelligent in a different way from the body cells at both Soul and Indigo level respectively.

When all Crystal cells are equally enlightened, there are no meridian lanes left in the body that distinguish themselves by being special messengers of holistic information between the body and the Spirit. Physical treatment methods using the meridian lanes in connection with a variety of healing and balancing systems are therefore no longer required.

This means that for certain types of body treatments that actively involve the meridian lanes' ability to convey energy to various places in the body, some changes must be made in the way those treatments are performed. Crystal Humans want to be treated where they have pain and not necessarily in other parts of their body that are presumed to correspond to the place that is in pain. In that regard Crystal Humans are very specific in their approach to both body treatments and life in general.

During the Body Crystallization Phase, when the Crystal cells are awakened and the meridian lanes slowly cease to exist, many Crystal Humans no longer benefit significantly from the treatment methods that used to enrich them. Instead, they need individual body treatments that do not necessarily follow the prevailing text books, which is why there will be a greater demand for capable, creative body therapists in the future, who are able to piece together some exciting, individual treatment solutions for their respective clients.

Once you are fully crystallized, the many acupuncture and pressure points of the body no longer work together through the meridian lanes in the body. Treatments such as acupuncture are therefore not able to impact at a meridian level in the Crystal body. On the other hand it is capable of affecting the Crystal body's organs and selected body areas more directly, e.g. through ear acupuncture.

Any body treatment that does not solely aim at affecting the body through the meridian lanes is therefore still effective. This is why reflexology, massage and acupressure etc. will continue to be among the alternative treatments of the future that will help to support the human body in a positive and balanced way.

Once you have been aura transformed it is even more important to find a good therapist that meets your needs and personal consciousness.

As long as the treatment remains at physical level and only involves physical treatment without the use of healing energy, you can easily choose to receive treatment from a non-aura transformed physiotherapist, massage therapist, etc. However, as soon as healing and energy balancing is part of the treatment, it is important that the body treatment is performed by someone who is aura transformed. Alternatively, you as a client run the risk of the therapist unknowingly slipping some healing energy into the treatment, which involves Soul Energy that represents an earlier phase in your own consciousness development process. Consequently many Crystal Humans and people who are in the midst of their Crystallization feel as if they are sent back in time. Often, after the treatment, their body and mind react by feeling limited in their development, which is definitely not to be recommended.

Drugs

During the Body Crystallization Phase many people respond much more intensely to tobacco, alcohol and drugs than normal. This is the reason why many people stop smoking and periodically refrain from drinking alcohol in connection with their Body Crystallization. For some, this happens already in connection with their AuraTransformation™.

Crystal Humans are not as focused on drugs as Indigo and Soul Humans can be. They enjoy the taste, the feeling and the physical sensation e.g. when they drink alcohol, but they are not aiming for a high. They are therefore focused on the enjoyment, rather than the drug. This is normally because their body not only becomes slightly affected by usual means of intoxication, but rather they can feel the high in their system – and unfortunately also the hangover – for several days after consumption.

Marijuana is completely detrimental for Crystal Humans' personal balance as well as their balance in respect of energy, which is why I strongly advise against smoking marijuana. The body literally feels crooked and completely out of balance for weeks after consumption, as it has great difficulty letting go of the effect of the intoxication right down to cell level. In addition, it feels like an extremely uneven fight for the body to find its way back to its original balance.

Young people, who are in the process of body crystallizing in particular will react severely to marijuana without noticing this themselves. It is very obvious to those in their environment that they are under the influence of something that makes them drowsy, as they seem inactive and become extremely unambitious - particularly in connection with agreements in their established everyday lives such as education, work and family relationships.

It is as if a hazy veil descends upon their entire personal charisma and consciousness that closes down the vision of reality, while causing a shift in their perception of time and place. It is suddenly 11 o'clock instead of 10 or 9 and they undeniably look at the watch in the same crooked way that their body and mind feel inside.

Changed needs

Many personal needs change concurrently with the change in body cell structure and aura structure. This happens when your aura is upgraded to Crystal Energy through an AuraTransformation™ and through the Crystallization of the cells in your body.

Strangely enough, the expression 'I normally…' disappears from your vocabulary, as nothing is the way it was before, which for the majority of people is most obvious in their relationships with friends and family and in their eating habits.

Case

Aura Mediator™ Kirstiin Suhrs, 53-year-old woman from Denmark describes her AuraTransformation™ and Crystallization Process as follows:

I was aura transformed by Anni (Sennov) in March 2005, the same year I turned 50. I came to Earth with a great deal of joy, self-will and drive, and an equal amount of physical and emotional vulnerability. Allergies and illnesses that required surgery made me aware of the environment, my diet and alternative treatment early on and I have been on a spiritual journey since I was very young. I didn't fit into the family I was born into, and moved far away from home when I turned 16. I felt alone, different and overlooked in my youth and although I was popular and attracted friends, my empathy with others caused me to adjust to their needs. My body was so sensitive that it collapsed in the end; for years I underwent one form of surgery after another and to the surprise of the doctors, I survived even the most extreme. I was usually alone in my views, my lifestyle seemed provoking, but I managed to live out my ideals while facing massive resistance, backstabbing and disrespectful treatment in my environment (worst of all from my relatives). I inspired, solved problems and got people going, but was never thanked for it. I lost my grounding during arguments and I was afraid to confront manipulative situations. Instead I defended myself by showing joy and bursting into laughter and thereby surviving time after time. It was a great success to watch my daughter grow up to become a strong, harmonious and talented woman, although my family had expected otherwise. Nobody was going to control me, but the anger that I hadn't let go of infected my body; an abscess behind my forehead contained no less than 17ml of infection!

My headline would be that my AuraTransformation™ and the Crystallization Process have been a rejuvenation cure that has helped me get rid of my physical ailments and disorders. My physical body has changed, emotionally and intellectually I have become free of locked behaviours and thought patterns - because it is all connected. I am feeling better and better, as if I had been born again, and I'm deeply grateful that Anni's book 'Crystal Children, Indigo Children & Adults of the Future' fell into my hands. A miracle has happened, but along the way I have endured life crises and strong physical and emotional reactions.

While my father was dying (he eventually died in December 2006), I spent a lot of time with him and we were able to heal our lives through insight and spiritual conversation. He had a near-death experience, which made him very clear and strong, despite the fact that his illness almost finished him off. My mother and my brother were far from happy about our developing closeness, my father was no longer compliant and he set his boundaries and showed anger. This brought out the worst in my mother and my brother and it resulted in several volcanic eruptions, and all the things that I hadn't said to them all my life, I now said straight to their face. I was not at the mercy of my feelings and felt anger and compassion at the same time, but everything had to come out. At the last clash with my mother I turned my back to her and was going to walk away from my childhood home for good. However, it never happened as my mother ran to me, fell on her knees and pleaded with me "please forgive me, please forgive me. I'll die, I'll take my life - I can't go on anymore." This was not a problem – my inner balance made me say, "yes", as if it were coming from my body. I didn't even think. She is now gentler, which is probably also because she is physically weak. She says that she's sorry that she was a bad mother and would do it differently if she could do it all over. It is actually as if my family has been transformed, although they have not had a consciousness expansion and a Balancing Body. The peculiar thing is that my mother always wears my clothes and my shoes. She loves hand-me-downs. Even at night she wears my old pyjamas and sleeps with my old sheets.

At the same time I let go of unhealthy relationships where I let myself be used – relationships that were not fulfilling; I was merely there to solve problems and keep people's spirits up. I established new relationships and joined groups that gave me a feeling of being equal and visible in a 'normal' way.

I had bouts of fatigue when I needed to lie down and the energies would vibrate in my body. Suddenly it would stop and I could continue to do whatever I was doing. Sometimes at night I couldn't move, the energies made my body stiff and there were noises inside my head, as if I were in the eye of a hurricane. Sometimes I fought to keep from getting sucked into the wall. This was when energy was pushed up through my lower body. It felt like a hand was pushing with all its strength.

Physically I coughed up mucus for almost two years - huge amounts. I used to be asthmatic and took asthma medication for 35 years. This is over now. It suddenly stopped and I no longer cough up mucus. My breathing is deeper and I can see from my iris analysis that my lungs are healing.

I have had some bad mouth sores in the mucus membranes of my mouth as well as dry, bright red and itchy eczema in both palms of my hands. The mucus membranes of my mouth have healed and the palms of my hands are almost healed as well. I also struggled with several eye infections, but it is all completely gone.

I have suffered from wind as well. Huge amounts. During my Crystallization I followed a Candida diet, did cleansing and took homeopathic drops. I have taken endless amounts of dietary supplements. However, resolution of the 'wind' problem took its time, but is now balanced. I got help from elm bark, Aloe Vera gel and intestinal flora bacteria in powder form. My latest initiative was to have a Vega test performed by an aura-transformed therapist. Through this treatment I am trying to heal my constitution at root level, i.e. from back in my childhood when the imbalances began and in my case it started with my lungs. I am now only taking one vitamin pill a day and EPA-GLA oil. My body is still sensitive and needs rest to regenerate and if I stuff myself with dietary supplements and drops, my energies will short-circuit and I will not benefit from the treatment.

I want to mention that after my AuraTransformation™ I didn't lean back and think that my life would now take care of itself. I always sought, fought and worked with myself and I continued to do so, but with renewed optimism. So many fortunate things are happening to me, I meet the right people, and then I don't need to think as much, because the 'right answers' spontaneously come to my mind in any situation when I need them, e.g. in dialogues or when I need to solve a problem. At night I have lucid dreams. My body is asleep but my consciousness is awake, and in dream-state I am able to ask my consciousness what the dream is about, and what it wishes to help me understand. I have integrated a sense of calm and an ability to be in the moment and enjoy life. I am not only fire-like, but have obtained a balance in all my body elements that serves me very well indeed. I feel protected and am no longer 'afraid' of people and their behaviour. I still need to spend a lot of time on my own and often walk 12-15 kilometres on the beach without being aware of it; I am simply in nature, getting close to and communing with birds, animals and trees..

"THE NEW TIME KIDS & PARENTS"

CHILDREN AND ADOLESCENTS OF THE NEW TIME

Children of the New Time are consciousness expanding

The big difference between children and adolescents of the past and the present is that children and adolescents of today are equipped with a much bigger and more powerful energy than their predecessors.

Due to the rapid expansion that is taking place in numerous societies around the world, many demands are today being placed on children and adolescents. However, just as many demands are placed on parents and adults who work with children and adolescents of the New Time. They are the ones who, each in their own field, must contribute to equipping the children to firstly become responsible adolescents and secondly to become responsible adults, who can each function as balanced individuals in society.

Preferably, the children of the New Time should already be able to function as good world citizens from childhood, who can manage their contact with anyone they meet in a balanced way, regardless of nationality and personal conviction. This is asking a lot of little people who are yet to grow into adults. On the other hand, this is a human quality that the children's own energy implies they must master at a young age. In the New Time, openness and acceptance of people's differences are personal qualities that you are required to have in a balanced world.

This is why nowadays many young children are playing well together in the playground, apparently without noticing each other's differences in race, clothing, culture, etc. Only when older siblings and/or parents are nearby to dictate the small children's attitude and behaviour do the children become dismissive towards other children, and people in general, who are different from their own cultural background.

Adult behaviour is a determining factor in the lack of openness that exists between foreign cultures today, as the parent generation - often without realizing it - passes down the separation of cultures to their children through their upbringing and influence.

At home, the parents set the agenda for the children's upbringing by influencing them through, e.g. a certain culture and/or denomination and with their personal opinions on life and the surrounding world. Only very few children are allowed to show the same openness, acceptance and sense of community towards their 'different' friends as they can towards their own family.

It can therefore be difficult for children to act out their own inner truth and show openness and acceptance towards others if they are influenced by their own parents to shut down towards anything that is foreign. This shutdown mechanism is one that the parents often practice to protect their children against danger and because they love them. This must however cause some internal conflict in the children's minds as to whether they are letting themselves or their parents down when they act a certain way.

It is a fact that all children and adolescents of the New Time are causing a consciousness expansion for their parents and the adults whom they associate with, whether or not the parents and the adults are aware of this.

Today's children and adolescents are generally open by nature, willing to learn and curious in a positive way. They are able to quickly familiarize themselves with a completely new way of thinking that they have never heard of before if they feel that it stimulates their mental consciousness. Most children therefore very quickly learn to play computer games, Nintendo DS™, PlayStation®, Wii™, etc. and many adolescents are all but experts in this, without requiring extraordinary assistance from their parents. As long as they get some basic guidance on how to start a game, most children and adolescents are capable of getting further by trying, or they get help from a friend or an adult to get ahead in the process.

For children and adolescents of the New Time only the goal matters, i.e. to learn to play the particular game and to complete it. It does not really matter to them if their parents or someone else helped them get through the game.

Most children and adolescents of the New Time have an inherent 'help gene' that is activated as soon as someone in their environment asks them for help. A help gene that may not be particularly visible to the parents when, for the tenth time they ask their children and adolescents to clear the table after dinner, if this is not already one of their regular chores around the house.

If this is a set daily chore of the children and adolescents, the parents do not even have to ask to have it done because the children and the adolescents will do this automatically without having to be reminded to do so over and over again. Helping your friends, parents or other adults comes very naturally for many children and adolescents as this helps build the community and therefore perfectly matches the children's and adolescents' holistic way of thinking. The more people that like the same kind of music and extracurricular activity or playing the same game, the more they have to talk about and do whenever they spend time together. This is again another aspect of the Crystal Energy's holistic mindset and essential structure that Indigo Children are also aligned with.

A lack of assistance and adult interest may have had a curbing effect for children with Soul Energy in the past, and may have often kept them from developing in a certain direction. Indigo and Crystal Children, however, refuse to be curbed by a lack of adult interest. Instead, they team up with their peers or with others, who have the same interests as they do and they live with the realization that their parents are unable to follow them in this area. As long as there is someone out there in society, with whom they can team up, their biological origin is not as important as it used to be. It is a sense of spiritual community that matters instead.

Confident and balanced parents notice right from when their children are little how they are able to live their lives completely independently of their parents, as long as they are fed and feel safe at home.

Today's children are consciously much more self-sufficient than they used to be, which enables them to form close relationships with their grandparents, uncles, aunts and friends at a very young age, as long as they know that everything at home that has to do with their family is the way it should be.

Security therefore means everything that gives the children courage to explore the world and team up with people other than their parents and at times, parents have to fight very hard to get their children's attention, just as they often have to fight to maintain their special status as parents, especially if everything is running smoothly at home and a family balance is prevalent.

Parents are therefore 'forced' to exceed their own boundaries and often also their own values, and be extra creative in order to attract their children's attention, which in itself is consciousness expanding. Since the children cannot be tempted with the same standard solutions as their parents were when they were children, that in itself places extraordinary demands on the parents' creativity. The family as a whole, however, can always attract the full attention of children and adolescents of the New Time, which is why they are sure to show up at family events if there is a general good atmosphere within the family.

The way today's young people socialize places great demands on their parents' personal and intimate set of values, because often the young people are crammed into someone's bed whenever they visit each other, without it damaging their sense of personal integrity. When they get up and leave to go to someone else's house, they repeat the exact same pattern of `interlacement`, without losing part of themselves or part of their energy along the way.

You see, with their Indigo and Crystal Energies they are able to stay true to themselves as whole individuals in any situation, regardless how comprehensive the fusion in each relationship is with a friend. They constantly interlace with other adolescents only to unlace again when it is time to move on and naturally it can be difficult for them to let go if they are 'just' going home to mum and dad, rather than a friend of equal energy. This is why the parents of today's children and adolescents must offer energy that is as equally attractive to them as that of their friends.

This can be done e.g. by the parents undergoing an AuraTransformation™ to match their children's consciousness energy to help them better 'read' their children's current needs. It does not have to happen by going to the movies, paintball or going skiing or by trying to outdo one trip with another - it is just as much a question of doing something that unites everyone and stimulates the family as a whole. Whether or not the parents are aura transformed, the more people who join the same trip, the more stimulating it is - particularly for the adolescents - as this gives them an opportunity to alternate between the energies that are present as they choose, without the risk of getting bored in the process.

Many parents and adults around the world are already very used to the quick and impromptu way of communicating in the New Time, which usually happens by mobile phone or computer. This is why these adults understand the youth's need for keeping their mobile phone at hand at all times, so that they will not feel alone.

Many parents and adults with Soul Energy, however, view this way of communicating as much too superficial and impersonal, which is why they often end up resenting the very manner of communicating that stimulates most adolescents in the best and most vivid way. In reality the adolescents are never alone when they carry their mobile phone (unless they choose to turn it off) which is exactly one of the main ideas behind project 'high-frequency communication at Earth level. You can always get in touch with someone out there, even on a boring, dark winter's night, therefore giving you a physical lifeline to the outside world. You can also always get in touch with someone if you are 'lost', either in your own mind or in a foreign city.

There may be a need for these adolescents to learn to be disciplined in how to specifically communicate with each other, through this media of our time, and it is up to each parent to handle this as part of their upbringing. It does not seem entirely responsible for a parent to be completely unaware of what their child is doing and whom they communicate with on a daily basis. Simply because it happens through these 'fast' lines of communication which constantly receive news, and where the news disappears just as quickly, does not mean that all communication is forgotten forever. This is why children and particularly adolescents must learn to consider what information it is that they share about themselves and others. The level of communication is high among today's adolescents and so is the amount of gossip, which is particularly prevalent among children and adolescents. These are young people who have not been educated by their parents on how to communicate through this media in a way that is considerate of yourself and others.

Today's chatting on mobile phones and computers can in many ways be compared to how neighbours used to chat over the fence. The big difference between then and now, however, is that communication is no longer limited to your neighbour. You can now just as easily talk to your friends at the other end of the country. Physical distance is no longer an obstacle for communicating with others as today's media offers countless cheap or free communication solutions.

This is why today many children and adolescents have friends who live far away and with whom they keep in touch for many years after meeting at an event, simply because they like each other. It used to be that that kind of friendship did not stand a chance of lasting in the long run, unless both parties kept in touch as pen pals, as the technology did not support the friend relationship back then. Responsible use of today's technology therefore has a very positive impact on the communication between the majority of all Indigo and Crystal Humans, as it contributes to making their everyday lives more practical and more spontaneously entertaining in many ways.

However, it is always the parents' responsibility to follow up on how their children are doing and how they communicate with their friends and others, so that they get used to showing respect and responsibility in everything they do.

So, in the Indigo and Crystal Phase, extraordinary demands are placed on all parents to really be familiar with their children's daily universe in order to get to know about them specifically and adolescents' physical reality and behaviour in society in general. Similarly, parents must be aware of their children's behaviour at school, amongst their friends and not least through mobile phones and computers, which are currently the fastest-vibrating communication channels that children and adolescents use.

If today's children and adolescents communicate a positive message to the outside world through a fast media, such as a mobile phone or a computer, it most often creates a positive and reaffirming response, but if they communicate a negative message, it may, due to their extreme force, damage themselves and others. It is crucial for parents of these children to be particularly aware of this.

It is about always being aware of what today's children and adolescents, with a strong consciousness, are doing and about

keeping an extra eye on them in the service of a greater good, although they may appear very balanced and self-sufficient.

Not until you, as a parent, are absolutely sure that your children can fully master a certain cause, are you able to leave the supervision of their actions to the children and the adolescents themselves. Until then, you must keep a constant eye on your kids in order to help them with the challenges of the outside world as much as possible. The fact that as a parent you are not always able to relax as much as you would either like or need to, is in many ways, the price you pay to be the parent of one of today's consciousness upgraded children, who believe they can do anything themselves.

Yes, they can do anything themselves, or almost, on a consciousness level, where they are often much stronger than their parents, but they are far from being able to do everything for themselves in the outside world. This is why as a parent you are often forced to mark your authority and greater knowledge when it comes to living in the physical dimension, by being extra strong in your own energy and really extending beyond your zone of influence in order to meet your children on the New Time territory. This is in itself, deeply consciousness-expanding and very demanding, especially if you are not tuned into the new, high-frequency Indigo and Crystal Energies that enable you to assert yourself with your strong, higher vibrational children.

An AuraTransformation™ is therefore recommended for all parents and other adults who associate with children and adolescents, and who have difficulty asserting themselves in relation to their own and other children. The consciousness standpoint of parents, and other primary caregivers prior to the transformation is of no importance whatsoever to the specific outcome of the AuraTransformation™. In a situation like that, the argument for choosing to become aura transformed is solely a question of maintaining your dignity and your self-esteem as a parent and an adult.

At consciousness level, the AuraTransformation™ also helps the parents signal more boundaries to the children, so that they sense that they can no longer fool their parents. There are additional consequences in the way the parents handle their children, when they live by the opinions they continue to express, so that their actions match their words. This is a language that children and adolescents understand.

Problem children are also consciousness expanding

Once things start to go wrong for today's powerful children and adolescents, the damage will be correspondingly greater and more extensive than previously.

Children and adolescents therefore need to associate with adults who are just as powerful as themselves and who know how to take the driver's seat and show them the best way through the earthly jungle.

Most parents of children who have been diagnosed with ADHD, ADD or DAMP (Deficits in Attention, Motor control and Perception), etc. are almost always guaranteed to contradict me when I state that the presence of various hyperactive reactional and behavioural patterns in children often happen in order to make their parents aware of these, to make them emotionally more conscious, and to expand their capacity as a human being.

The presence of hyperactive children in their parents' lives, however, can also be to activate their parents' life missions, particularly if it is part of their Dharma to work with children in either diagnosis of, or alongside, children and adolescents of the New Time as e.g. teachers, counsellors, therapists, researchers and spokesmen and women in a variety of contexts.

If instead, these children were born to a different type of parents, who were a better match energy-wise, the problem with hyperactive children would often not occur in the same way. These parents, who have the 'pleasure' of their hyperactive children on a day-to-day basis, would not have the option of letting go of their inherent value judgements, either, and would perhaps never have the opportunity to move their consciousness mentally, emotionally or physically. Parents of problem children are forced to put themselves beyond their own needs, and open up considerably to alternative solutions in their lives in the hope of being better able to handle their uncontrollable children. If daily life is very stressful, you are often very open to any innovation that can ease your own experience specifically and everyday life in general. This is the exact purpose of the presence of the most difficult children in their parents' lives, i.e. to teach the parents and the family to think in new and different ways.

Nothing is as consciousness expanding for today's parents as having sick and problematic children who are awake much of the night, as only very few parents are willing to leave their 'little sweethearts' with relatives overnight to get some peace and quiet, and possibly some more sleep. So in situations like that, parents often make huge sacrifices in order for their children to feel better and safer because the parents' innate 'care gene' tells them to do so, no matter how old their children are.

If, on the other hand, something were wrong with great-grandmother, she would in most cases be left with 'paid care', leaving children and grand-children with a reasonably good conscience, if the elderly person had been sick for a long time. The biggest and most determining difference in the children's and the great-grandmother's presence in the parents'/adults' lives is that the children are here at the parents' instigation and request. The children therefore have much greater leverage with the parents when it comes to challenging their tolerance and perseverance, in a way that the great-grandmother and other adults in the family do not have.

ADHD and DAMP is not as prevalent in Crystal Children as it is among Indigo Children. While Crystal Children who love to be surrounded by harmony and lightness, including sounds, most Indigo Children have a great need to surround themselves with many loud sounds to activate mental fluctuations in their brain and to even be able to think. These are sounds that most adults perceive as noise, but that Indigo Children perceive as stimulation.

Once they have stimulated their mental energy, so that they have an in-ner feeling of functioning and being in 'high gear', adult management is urgently required to turn the noise level back down. Just as boxers are accompanied by stimulating, powerful music when they enter the boxing ring, the music is turned down once the fight begins.

The noise only serves as a kick-starter to increase the frequency and to get going. After that the adults - and in the boxing ring, the referees - need to have a general overview of their children's everyday lives, the current situation, and be able to draw the line on how things are allowed to develop in their children's activity universe regarding structure, chores, sleep, eating habits, breaks, fun, etc.

It is always the parents' responsibility to raise their children according to the time we live in. It is therefore also the parents' responsibility to keep an overview of their children's lives and activities, which New Time children, with their high level of activity, are very good at forcing their parents to do. These children need constant stimulation in their lives, so that they are able to convert their energy capacity appropriately. On the other hand, if too much is going on all at once, the children will often have difficulty being in their own energy and tolerating themselves. This is a rather difficult balance to manage, and one, which Crystal Children are much better at handling than Indigo Children. Indigo Children need additional stimulation in the form of action and activity, which is why it is recommended that parents include elements with large physical activity, competition, noise and fast pace as part of their daily or weekly schedule.

If Indigo Children cannot convert their energy properly and constructively on an ongoing basis and if there is no parental and/or adult supervision, things can go terribly wrong for these children. The amount of power and energy that these children possess does not belong at the lower end of the energy scale, which unfortunately many parents and adults do not quite understand.

They 'simply' believe that their children represent an ex-

tended version of themselves, which in some ways may be true. Unfortunately, they do not also see that their beloved children have energy that corresponds to that of an entire nuclear bomb in their consciousness, where the parents only had a consciousness energy corresponding to a regular bomb when they were children themselves.

Throughout the entire Indigo Phase from the mid 1980s up until now, there has been a significant shift in the consciousness of all newborn children who, during that period of time, were born as little, living Pinocchio's without any strings to control their actions.

All Indigo Children are born with a consciousness of having escaped from Pinocchio's father Gepetto's strings and fate-controlled Soul consciousness. They are therefore free to move about within the Spirit and the matter here on Earth as they choose, which places additional demands on Gepetto's attention as a responsible father. Who knows what Pinocchio might do when moving about on his own in the big bad world without sufficient knowledge of the dangers?

The consciousness levels in most people have therefore changed much more than the outer elements, which is particularly evident in all children and adolescents when something goes wrong or when a singing sensation is born and suddenly reaches the top of the world's music charts at the young age of 15.

The energy can either carry these adolescents right into Heaven or straight to Hell if they make the wrong choices in their lives, which is how it is for people of the New Time to live with their own free will while having to take responsibility for their own actions. Interestingly enough, the majority of today's Indigo adolescents do not wish that things were different, as they cannot comprehend being subject to outside authorities in either Spirit or matter. They are good at acting out their wishes and at realizing their visions. They would rather seek God within themselves than listen to the various wise people around them, although it may not always seem that way. This is why they generally do not like adults, particularly if adults try to discipline them, unless the adults have proven to the adolescents that they are quick thinking and good at talking back and know the hot keys on the keyboard. Equal expression creates respect among young Indigos, whereas Crystal Children generally respect all adults, regardless of the extent of their consciousness capacity.

Parents of the majority of today's adolescents can therefore choose to be parents based on their own needs or that of the adolescents. If they choose the former, they run the risk of getting some big surprises along the way in connection with their children's upbringing, as many new potential problem areas have surfaced that did not exist when they were children and adolescents themselves.

If instead the parents choose to become updated with respect to their energy through an AuraTransformation™ in order to better match their personal energy with that of the adolescents, it will become noticeably easier for them to relate to the adolescents' universe productively and appropriately. With a more conscious and goal-oriented parental support of adolescents, they first and foremost become better able to function and balance. Subsequently they get better at making goal-oriented and suitable choices in their life than if their parents had not met their needs and supported them.

The decision to have your aura transformed to better meet your 'impossible' children's personal needs, and those related to this new energy, usually comes up for many parents when their children are in trouble. This happens because the need for assistance in obtaining a more balanced relationship between themselves and their children is so big, and perhaps even acute, that they are willing to do almost anything to help their children. They will even undergo an AuraTransformation™ that will make them focus their attention on how they live their own lives - a decision that, in a situation like that, often helps the parents just as much as it helps the children, although it was circumstances surrounding the children that made the parents decide to undergo an AuraTransformation™.

General information
on Children of the New Time

Many children and adolescents are unique and pleasant beings when they are within the right framework. They can, however, be true devils in other situations when 'proper' adults are not there to balance them and set boundaries for them.

Therefore much depends on the adults' ability to assert and set boundaries for themselves, the children and adolescents, and for the time they spend together.

If parents believe that they are good parents because they let their children do anything they want, I truly believe they are awfully mistaken. This may make it easier for them to get through the child rearing years when most parents usually keep an extra eye on their children. However, to leave all child rearing and boundary setting to other adults and society in general, while also leaving it to the children to find their own way through the earthly social and behavioural jungle with no parental support, is simply irresponsible.

You cannot even call it 'free child rearing'. Instead, it is *lack* of child rearing.

Children and adolescents need guidance although this does not mean that you need to talk about everything. Today's pushy children and adolescents especially need guidance in how to behave reasonably in society, so the parents carry a great responsibility of looking after their children's development in a positive and current way.

In this way, society will always be a little behind the times regarding adolescent needs, as the adults themselves have created the framework for these opportunities of expression for today's children and it is not easy to change this. Many generations have to live side by side on this Earth which is why it is important that young people are taught also to make room for the way in which the elderly relate to the world.

Children and adolescents must learn to make room for adults of all ages and varieties, so that they do not automatically expect the adult generation to be there, just for them. Many pushy Indigo Children might think so, once they put the skids under their own parents and get their way in every situation, simply because the parents do not have the energy to fight their children. Unfortunately, such children have no problem overruling statements of other adults, because they have already won their first match on home turf. They now fight to win additional matches away from home, but with what outcome? No one likes this type of child, whose number has gradually increased throughout the Indigo Period because their Soul-based parents were irresponsible and afraid to set boundaries for the children and to stick to their decisions. Sad, but unfortunately true!

All children of the New Time ought to be equipped with a small portion of basic human knowledge from home and a standard behaviour of courtesy and friendliness when they enter into the world on their own. This can be compared to people observing traffic regulations and adults adhering to company policies in order for the surrounding environment to function optimally and be clear to all involved parties.

These factors make perfect sense to Crystal Children without their parents having to explain why. In fact, most of them automatically ask about the rules of the outer world at a very young age so that they can be well prepared when venturing into the world on their own.

Crystal Children are generally very compliant and find it natural to behave properly and politely towards others. Naturally, they need to go through the same physical and psychological development phases as Indigo Children and children at Soul level when they say bad things and anxiously anticipate the harmful and surprised reaction of adults, etc. but all of this happens in a more balanced way than it did with Indigo Children.

The difference in energy between Indigo and Crystal Children is described in my book 'Crystal Children, Indigo Children & Adults of the Future' of 2004, which has been translated into several languages. The human difference between these two kinds of children, however, is described as follows:

In appearance Crystal Children generally seem somewhat more sophisticated, delicate and colourless than Indigo Children, which is not as apparent in children with golden or dark skin and in children with fair skin when summer arrives and they get a tan. Their personality is generally very friendly and non-judgmental. However, do not be mistaken, they can be very sharp, articulate and straightforward in their statements and if they feel the need to say something, this is done without consideration for the recipient, who will be served the pure truth directly on a platter and without accompaniment.

Indigo Children are often either charismatic or defiant in their expression. They seem more simplified and one-sided in the way they express themselves than Crystal Children and at times they may even make rude statements. If they wish to either accomplish something or explain something away, you often get an either/or explanation from them in the hope that you as an adult will approve of one of the explanations. Indigo Children come across as very pushy or often somewhat rude, transgressive and/or curious in their facial expression and their eyes, whereas Crystal Children seem more friendly and gentle while at the same time being very clear and direct in their facial expression, particularly their eyes.

Crystal Children are very fairness-minded in their associations with other children and they quickly involve adults if there is conflict because that is what they have learned to do.

Indigo Children are also very fairness-minded, but do not always clearly see their own involvement in a given social situation. Once they have had a chance to speak up about what is on their mind, they are not always motivated to hear what is on the mind of others. Their sense of fairness can in many ways be equated with the freedom of speech, where they have the right to speak themselves. Whether their environment has the same right to speak does not really matter too much in this context. They talk about fairness, but this means fairness as seen from their corner of the boxing ring.

The fact that Indigo Children can be particularly rough and tyrannical to each other is not always experienced as a problem by them, as their form of expression is very physical, while they have the spiritual aspect pinpointed in their aura, which gives them good intuition. This is why young Indigos in particular have a great need to touch each other all the time and walk hand-in-hand without necessarily dating. They love it when several young people lie closely together when they hang out and even choose to sleep under the same cover, just to have a chance to sleep in the same bed. Like animals, they are in very close, direct contact with their physical body, which is why their body language is often very simplified and easy to understand for the outside world.

Like all young animals, they can easily share their plate so in that respect they are very sociable and can always fit one more into the group if that individual matches the existing group energy. If there is no spot available, they will make one anyway. If, however, the outsider deviates significantly from the group's energy, they are not always as willing to let him or her in - because it is all about balance in the existing group. On the other hand, the individual members of the group may easily get together with the 'outsider' at other times, because it is then a completely different balance that needs to be considered, i.e. the balance between two individuals, rather than that of an entire group.

In a way you can say that today's parents have much more help in their daily contact with their children than parents did previously, if they choose to go through the trouble of reading their children's clear body language and changing facial expressions. No parent today can doubt, whether their children are hungry, tired or happy, as the signalling of Indigo Children is visible to everyone.

With their focus on their physical body and the direct influx of Spiritual Energy, which unfortunately does not always cooperate optimally but follows each other closely, the Spiritual Energy places great expectations on Indigo Children to spend their childhood and adolescence learning to become balanced Crystal Individuals. Of course they need to have fun while they are children and adolescents, but in addition to focusing on obtaining a balance in their life, they all have a great life mission in teaching their parents a great deal about spirituality and human values and about boundary setting as one of the Crystal Energy's virtues.

As years go by, Indigo Children solve their respective life missions by awakening selected people in their, at times, sluggish and narrow-minded environment. The spiritual aspect automatically evolves in their own physical bodies through which they body-crystallize and subsequently automatically acquire their Crystal aura. In this way, even more Crystal Children and Crystal Adults are constantly entering this world than all the mothers in the world are physically able to give birth to. Whether it is Crystal Children or Crystal Adults who are 'born' solely depends on how old the Indigos are when they are fully crystallized. So, to be very optimistic, you could say that Indigo Children aim to grow out of their, at times, primitive and violent behaviour, as in no way does this belong in the Crystal universe since they do not stand a chance of fully crystallizing if they are either internally, physically and spiritually unbalanced.

Crystal Children will always try to find a balance between seriousness and joy in their everyday lives, which is a signal to the outside world that, in reality, they are little adults in children's bodies. This is why many of them can become acquainted with the conditions in the real world from a very young age, simply because they ask questions themselves and want truthful answers. The children may not be aware of the fact that many parents try to present reality to their children in a way that does not seem too dangerous while they are very young. However, children will make sure to have their many questions answered very quickly if they feel that they were not sufficiently informed by their parents, teachers, etc., in which case TV and the Internet can be very helpful. In addition, they sense very clearly if someone tries to make them believe something that is not quite true. It is better to tell them that they are too young to hear about it and that you will discuss it with them when they are older. That is much easier for them to relate to - because it is the truth.

For example, many Crystal Children know from a very young age that Santa Claus is not for real, but they love to fantasize about him living somewhere on the North Pole - because it is no problem for them to hear the truth behind the fairytale, which to them is often more interesting than the fantasy itself. So, in that respect Crystal Children are pretty tough to deal with, as they do not want to be tricked by adults who are trying to tell them a story in any respect. On the other hand, they can easily keep a secret if it seems appropriate and truthful. If there is something sneaky about it, though, they will tell it, which can help detect potential abuse at an early stage and probably prevent it from taking place over a long period of time in the Crystal Energy. This is an inherent quality that makes most parents and other adults feel particularly safe about Crystal Children.

While writing the two books *'The Crystal Human and the Crystallization Process Part I'* and *'Part II'* some people have asked me, whether Indigo Children have a hidden or shady side, but I do not perceive it as such at all. On the contrary! All sides of them are highly visible, including the ugly sides. Shady sides are often unconscious sides of yourself that you do not really know how to handle and cannot always relate to. Indigo Children, however, always know themselves, whether or not they act like jerks towards friends and family. They just do not always know why they are the way they are, which is where adult support is needed to help them understand the context and help them behave more appropriately.

It often only takes a good deal of boundary setting and insight from adults to change the situation, but unfortunately many adults around the Indigo Children are not always willing to acknowledge the children's devilry. Or, they simply do not have the strength to get involved in the children's and the young Indigos' constant problems and perhaps subconsciously hope that things will work out by themselves, which they rarely do. This is why it can be difficult to fight off Indigo Children's sometimes-rude behaviour once and for all, because no adults really take their time to make a difference in the children's lives to change things.

If an Indigo Child e.g. notices a sense of indifference in one of his or her parents (including where the parents are divorced and the child lives permanently with the parent who is not indifferent) the indifference can easily shine through in the Indigo Child because the child always reflects his or her environment, especially that of their close family. If there is an inappropriate influence from an older sibling that the parents have not detected, the Indigo Child will make sure that this influence is made visible through their behaviour at some point. This is why the behaviour of Indigo Children can truly be the foundation for Soul-searching between the parents, even if (and especially if divorced) the parents do not always agree which of the parties needs to change their respective behaviour and mindset.

However, it can just as easily be step parents, friends or others who, without realizing it, contribute to setting the agenda for the Indigo Child's behaviour, as children of the New Time, i.e. Indigo Children and Crystal Children pick up influence anywhere. They are supposed to learn to balance themselves, both in the earthly layers and in the heavenly layers, which thankfully is rarely a problem for Crystal Children who perceive them as one united world.

Indigo Children, on the other hand, have difficulty bringing the two worlds together at times – the earthly and the heavenly – which at an energy level is separated in their body and their aura with the Balancing Body as its mediator and translator. This is why they are not always able to see the big picture in the same way that Crystal Children do. They either see the world from ground level or they choose to view it from above without having both feet planted firmly on the ground in the real world. This is an either-or situation which all Indigo Children must balance in their system before it is possible for them to have their aura upgraded from an Indigo to a Crystal aura while crystallizing in their body.

The physical reality of children and adolescents

Looking at the world today, it can be very difficult for many adults to imagine how life will turn out for children and adolescents in the future - because for each new generation, adolescents behave more and more maturely and at a younger age than the previous generation, although they are definitely not. Furthermore, the fun that the majority of adolescents surround themselves with at night is becoming increasingly more dangerous and transgressive than the fun of the past.

Today it is therefore not unusual for parents of adolescents to agree to, or end up having to accept the fact that their half-grown children come home with piercings and tattoos on their bodies and have tried this and that sexually, which their parents knew nothing about at all when they were young. This happens because the adolescents want to sexually explore all the cavities in their bodies and decorate themselves and their physical bodies as much as possible, which particularly characterizes the Indigo Phase.

It is simply because the more you show your body to the outside world, the better you feel inside - because they have nothing to hide in their consciousness, and they have no hidden agendas, so why should they hide anything about their physical body? Since most Indigos like lying, sitting or standing closely to others whom they like, they have no problem e.g. exploring each other's intimate body cavities in each other's company when they have sex. They have no need to hide behind lights that are turned off at all whenever they have sex, not even if they are merely 12-15 years old when they make their sexual debut, which thankfully is not the standard for all Indigo Children and Indigo Adolescents. In addition they can talk about anal sex and consumption of drugs at an incredibly young age, and completely out of proportion with the world that their actual age belongs to.

Today it is possible for children of all ages with a TV and a computer in their home, especially if the TV and the computer is in their own room and away from parental supervision, to watch 'hot stuff' while a vast number of music and youth shows are showing on TV. Shows that have not seen the light until the Indigo Period and that therefore have an extraordinary focus on body and Spirit in a slightly revised version consisting of suggestive dance and hot, inspiring music.

While the younger children are flicking the many TV channels to find a good or funny children's movie they can relax to, they can suddenly come across youth-oriented information on sex, dating, relationships, drugs and youth crime that apparently are 'topics of the day' on a youth channel, and whose target group is definitely not young children.

The young children might also come across a music channel with lots of young, hot, scantily dressed music stars - often female - exposing themselves and moving their bodies in very suggestive, provocative positions. If the music is good, the children usually stay on the channel until the song is over and during this time they have more than enough opportunity to study the singer's physical presentation of the song. So, just how do you think these young children choose to do the hot music performance next time they show up at the song contest at their school or after-school care, unless their caregivers manage to stop them in time?

Children of today are, in this way, easily able to have their incessant curiosity for life and other people satisfied, simply by watching TV or being on the computer all day. There are no questions they cannot find an answer to there – questions that they have not even thought about themselves.

When it is about acquiring knowledge on life and the surrounding world, many of today's Indigo Adolescents can easily live without the presence of their parents, which is why the phenomena, such as independent boarding schools, youth camps, etc. will gradually increase in popularity as years go by. Such institutions and group environments can stimulate adolescents into learning much more in a short time than they

would at home, simply because there are many activities and lots going on all the time.

What the Internet, independent boarding schools and various camps cannot provide adolescents of today with is a good and lasting personal influence with a loving touch that teaches the adolescents to not just be energetic and active all the time, but to also be able to rest in themselves and to feel safe and close in their personal relations. Indigo relations between adolescents are very open and honest, but not always particularly loving.

Children of today, i.e. Indigo Children and Crystal Children have no problem showing themselves and their many talents to the world, including in various competitions, because if they believe they are talented themselves, the rest of the world is sure to agree, which however is far from true in the real world. However, this is something that many young Indigos will realize themselves when they grow up and travel the world more and as the Crystal Energy gradually gains ground in societies around the world. Fortunately, the majority of today's adolescents are able to use their intuition far more than the majority of adults, so once they have experienced that the world did not agree with them in a certain matter, they will automatically keep a lower profile next time around, because today's young people are no fools – they know how to adjust to their environment. However, the big challenge for children of the New Time, particularly the Indigo Children, is that they often take a starting point in life that is a bit too self-confident, where they trust their own spiritual immortality so much that they completely forget to consider the physical aspects of the real world, which is highly mortal. If you mess this up, it will not be forgotten tomorrow like it would in the spiritual world where the energy is more momentary.

For example, if a child is a good actor, this is no guarantee that the child can also sing well, which Indigos in particular sometimes have a hard time accepting, as they often believe they are good at everything. This is because only when they have arrived at the Crystal level are they able to access their Dharma deep down at cell level in their body to gain clarity of their exact life mission.

In the Crystal universe each Crystal Individual looks after their very own life mission in the earthly matrix, and it is their responsibility and no-one else's. There can therefore easily be 500,000 healers or bookkeepers in the world, but they act as such in their local area within their own field and each in their own way.

In addition to having to learn to relate to the spiritual and physical world as one, there are many external factors in Indigo Children's lives that can easily play a more or less balancing part for them in the journey towards their Body Crystallization and towards becoming upgraded in their aura. There are still many parents who get divorced where the Indigo Children need to find a balance between their own inner and outer energies and values. They also need to find a personal balance within themselves and in the outside world between their divorced parents' respective energies and worlds, if they are still in touch with both of them after the divorce. If the children are only in touch with one of the parents after the divorce, it is actually easier for them to relate to the world, as there is only one immediate player to play with and balance with, i.e. the lone parent. If the children are in contact with both parents after the divorce, which most children are, this can particularly help stimulate Indigo Children in a positive way, as they generally enjoy getting lots of different input on a regular basis, which may also be more confusing than beneficial.

In a divorce situation it is therefore the parents' number one job to make sure they take their children into account as much as possible when making agreeing access arrangements. Some Indigo Children feel best if they are able to come and go as they please in both parents' homes without fixed agreements, whereas others need set agreements on when to be with whom for a certain number of days at a time in order to function as well as possible.

Sometimes the parents' work situations determine the outcome of the visitation agreement and the children are not able to influence the conditions themselves. In such cases the parent who works a lot or is frequently away on business trips must try to compensate in different ways, e.g. by having an extended holiday with the children or by making it extra entertaining when he or she does have the opportunity to spend time with the children so that the absence does not feel as big for either party.

What matters most in relation to Indigo Children and Indigo Adolescents and divorce or parent absence is that the children's and adolescents' needs are always met as much as possible when a divorce or other kinds of parent absence occur in their everyday lives. Indigo Children are very flexible and cooperative when it comes to solutions for the home, as long as there is openness and transparency in connection with parental access and decision-making. The goal is simply to make it as easy as possible for the children to follow the development of their parents, without the children having to completely give up their own interests, friends, etc. As long as there is some recognition of the way things used to be, Indigo Children can easily adjust to a new framework and new conditions.

The same applies to Crystal Children who however do not always choose to be as flexible as Indigo Children, as Crystal Children have an inner route that they must follow - and if this route is best followed by living with one of the parents, this will be the solution. Crystal Children are not good at travelling back and forth between two parents, unless this is part of their Dharma.

Children of the New Time are generally healthy but, because they are constantly rubbing against others, holding other people's hands and walking so closely together that their hair almost gets tangled, and in addition cough and spit and sometimes get so aggressive that their saliva flies from their mouths when they speak, there is a great risk of catching various kinds of viruses.

In alternative circles many therapists and clients naturally conclude that when a person catches a certain virus or infection, this happens because the person needs to cleanse their body and their consciousness and to become upgraded with respect to their energy. However, it is important to note that children of the New Time do not always catch infections and viruses because they need to have their energy upgraded with a view to crystallize in their aura and their body. Once in a while the children and adolescents simply need peace and calm in order for them to gather their own energies - a process that happens best and most quickly when they are on their own or at home with their parents.

In relation to children of the New Time and their health, the physical aspect should not be considered in isolation. Many of today's children associate with adults who have the Old Time Soul Energies in their auras, and these children cannot help but be influenced by this. Therefore, you also need to consider their consciousness just as much. This influence may well be suitable at a mental and a human level but, at a consciousness level, it can often pull the children and adolescents' energy down so that they themselves then have to fight to increase their energy.

Unfortunately, there are only two safe ways for most children of the New Time to rebuild their energy on their own, if their environment has drawn them too far down.

This is by either developing a fever and losing consciousness control of their body, which makes the Spiritual Energy completely take over, or by teaming up with their friends and making trouble, so that the adrenaline gets going in their body.

Both methods are equally uncomfortable, which is why it is even more important for the parents to learn to understand the principles behind balancing as well as integrating the Spiritual Energy in their children's physical and energetic bodies as this is a process that all Indigo Children and Indigo Adolescents need to go through at some point in order to become fully crystallized in their aura and body.

Those parents, whose children use the first two methods to increase their own energy again when they have been subject to Old Time Energy for too long, should actually not complain too much. Certainly not if they compare themselves to parents of children who have been diagnosed with ADHD, ADD or DAMP, which is given to children with significant concentration and focus difficulties – and there are many of those children around the world.

Children and adolescents with the above-mentioned diagnoses all have difficulty handling the pure Spiritual Energy's penetration into their already hyperactive and mobile children's body and brain. They often lack physical density in their physical and consciousness system to help them create physical closeness and consciousness presence wherever they are at a given time. You can easily compare children with ADHD, ADD and DAMP, etc. to air balloons. Not air balloons that are about to take off, but rather air balloons that are already up in the air and do not know how to land because they do not have a good place to land. In addition, they cannot always see the purpose in landing.

These unfocused, hyperactive children can be helped in several ways, for example, by surrounding them with good, old-fashioned human and physical values, such as calm, cleanliness and regularity. This will enable the children to gradually learn to fit into the more earthy consciousness framework than those they are surrounding themselves with in their spiritual consciousness. It is also beneficial to have the children's vitamin and mineral imbalances checked as well as potential allergies towards foods, detergents, vaccines, etc.

It is also recommended to check if the children have large deposits of metal in their body, in which case a metal detoxification could be a solution. Last but not least parents must be careful not to let their children consume too much sugar, such as in candy, soft drinks and juice, as the sugar really gets hyperactive children going. Even fructose can have the same effect on the children, which is why it is better for them to eat foods such as vegetables.

Children who have been diagnosed with OCD (Obsessive-Compulsive Disorder), who suffer from compulsive thoughts and actions thus need calm, cleanliness and regularity, as these human and structured values slowly but surely can help them gather the courage to take on new challenges in their everyday lives. As the children start to feel safe when repeating the above-mentioned challenges, these are gradually incorporated into their daily routine, which is mainly based on selected security actions.

For children and adolescents who have been diagnosed with these various conditions, the exact same criteria apply as to all other children of today, as they are very easy to read for their environment. If they have comprehension and behavioural difficulties, it is obvious to everyone and therefore something can be done about it. There are few children in modern societies here on Earth today who do go without help for very long at time. If so, that would indicate that something is wrong with the social conditions, which not only harms the children who have difficulty focusing and learning, but also all other people in that particular society. Most countries

---

Fortunately, all Indigo Children of today and all future Crystal Children each have their own divine impulse deep down at cell level in their own physical bodies, regardless of their childhood conditions. This impulse will, when the time is right, help them find the right path through the earthly jungle to their Dharmaic destination where they are expected to act out their respective life missions.

So, perhaps along the way they were affected negatively by their Soul-oriented parents and the surrounding society, but when children of the New Time discover something that seems more right than what they knew previously, they all have the ability to change direction when the timing feels right for them. Since Crystal Humans cannot lie to themselves, and at the same time they follow their inner clock, without knowing the exact time, they instinctively know when it is time to do certain things in their lives.

So, once all Crystal Individuals discover a new truth, they just wish to live out this truth, at any cost - personal and financial.

Naturally it will slow down the general development here on Earth since not all children of the New Time are lucky enough to have consciousness updated parents with a strong energy and a good perspective. AuraTransformation™ and similar consciousness expanding methods, of course, do not yet reach all corners of this Earth to help all parents integrate the Crystal Energy into their aura and thereby meet their children at a consciousness equal level.

This only means that the development in some areas of the world will be delayed when it comes to updating the Crystal Energy at society level. On the other hand, we will have an opportunity to see entire areas that used to be poor or behind in social and technological development suddenly skip a few consciousness development stages and move straight into the Crystal Energy. Perhaps with a 20-30-year delay compared to other countries, but in return they will have managed to catch up on several hundreds of years of development in just a few decades. Africa will therefore enjoy its heyday in the future regarding consciousness development, comparable to that of e.g. Egypt at its peak.

The way things are developing in the earthly dimension is how things also develop in the smaller human picture around today's Indigo Children and Indigo Adolescents. These young people surround themselves with parents and other adults at Soul level, because these children and adolescents do not always receive the help and support they need throughout their childhood and their youth. On the other hand, once they are adults themselves, they will know what children and adolescents of the Third World need in order to become more balanced individuals, so that it will become easier for them to open up to various new, progressive mindsets and lifestyles of more developed parts of the world. In some way, those of today's Indigo Children and Indigo Adolescents who were not fortunate enough to pull their parents' consciousness to a level where they decided to become aura transformed, will end up working with conditions in their respective adult lives in which they will need the exact life experience that they are bringing along in their personal baggage.

Some life experience is best learned the hard way, and for physically oriented Indigo Children and Indigo Adolescents, various learning experiences often must be knocked into their heads with a sledge hammer for them to remember and understand, as they need to incorporate their physical intelligence, i.e. to activate their physical memory just as much as involving and activating their brain.

Thoughts and invisible communication between people

Invisible communication takes place between all people. In this book, however, I have chosen to focus on the relationship between adults and children and adolescents, in order to help parents better understand the consciousness motives behind many children and adolescents', at times, inexplicable behaviour when they are together with certain people.

People's communication consists of much more than words and body language.

People can also communicate with their charisma, which contains all information about the individual's thoughts and emotions as well as psychological and physical condition, etc. This charisma can be read by all people and animals through simple use of intuition and/or instinct.

Fortunately for today's children and adolescents and for aura-transformed adults, others cannot enter into their Indigo and Crystal aura if they have not been invited to do so. Children, adolescents and aura-transformed individuals may, however, choose to open up to external conditions that may take over more than anticipated, in which case they must regain their balance as quickly as possible. This can happen in many ways - either through reflection, relaxation, conscious focus or through massage or Balancing sessions by an Aura Mediator™.

Under normal circumstances, however, other people do not affect them with their respective thoughts and emotions and other kinds of manipulation, even from a distance, which is otherwise possible in Soul Land. So in that way, children, adolescents and all aura-transformed adults avoid external penetration into their own system, which however does not keep them from reacting to other people's unexpressed thoughts and emotions that are hidden behind the respective people's aura.

Children of the New Time generally communicate very clearly with others, although Indigo Children and Indigo Adolescents in particular are not very good at reaching final decisions. This has nothing to do with lack of clarity though, as they thereby show their parents, teachers, friends and others just how difficult it is for them to make a decision on a given matter. The children willingly stand by their own indecisiveness and if parents want to teach them the importance of making a final decision about something in order to show respect for their surroundings, this can easily be done.

In many ways children of the New Time are very tolerant regarding the needs of others, so if their parents want structure in order to be able to better plan things around the house, that is how things are going to be. If their friends cannot decide whether or not to hang out together, they take things as they come without planning themselves to death.
You could say that children and adolescents let the inspiration, the Spirit and the unstructured part of themselves decide the course, which mostly applies to Indigo Children and Indigo Adolescents. Crystal Children and Crystal Adolescents like to be more in control of things so that they can get as much done as possible in the shortest time possible. Through their combined physical and spiritual structure, they manage to incorporate the impulsive and creative Spiritual Energy into everything they do as a fully integrated part of their predestined life.
Clear signalling is a high priority for the Indigo as well as the Crystal Energies and children and adolescents of the New Time react very negatively and distance themselves when adults apply `invisible signalling` and use body language, rather than words, to show their surroundings whether they are satisfied or dissatisfied with certain things.

What many adults do not know is that as humans we use our thoughts and emotions to express our sympathy, antipathy and neutrality towards our environment and that these thoughts

and emotions are very easy to read in people's auras.

Thoughts and emotions of Indigo and Crystal Humans are also easy to read in their body language, which they are not always aware of themselves.

Thoughts represent an introverted process that is only expressed if the person chooses to vocalise his or her thoughts.
Emotions usually represent an introverted as well as an extroverted process, as it can be difficult to keep your emotions pent-up for very long. Emotions are a more action-oriented expression than thoughts and if the thoughts get the upper hand, the process has the ability to be more balanced because the expression is then controlled.

You can read the behaviour of others through their body language and through the signals they send out when they are active. Passive people, however, do not send out signals, which is why people around them often have to use their physical vision as their only means of perception when trying to relate to passive people. In such cases, the only parameters for orientation are based on looks, clothes and possibly speech.

Animals, children and sensitive adults often pick up on other people's invisible signalling through thoughts and emotions without reservation and they usually act in the same way - without reservation - to the signals they pick up on by becoming either aggressive, sad or happy.

People who are not in touch with themselves, but who either consciously or subconsciously have many thoughts and emotions in relation to their environment, which they either wish to keep to themselves or are incapable of expressing, often have a powerful invisible signalling mechanism towards their environment. Unfortunately for themselves and the people around them, they are not aware that the environment is able to pick up on their innermost feelings and emotions, which animals, children and sensitive adults always can.

Animals, children and sensitive adults usually do not judge their fellow beings based on exterior factors, such as looks, clothes, provable intelligence, etc. and due to their very openness and their lack of boundary setting, they often act as catalysts for people in their proximity, who are unable to express their own thoughts and emotions themselves. This happens for example through children or sensitive adults suddenly expressing a thought or concept, or acting in a certain way that is completely out of context with what is going around them and for the company they are in. The explanation for this is often in the hidden signalling that is taking place around them and which Soul people in particular are good at acting out without always realizing it themselves.

Most often it is our view and our thoughts - i.e. primarily the mental part of our consciousness - that interpret the impressions we receive from our surroundings. The body as a whole also has various energy sensors that it can use, as it runs on certain frequencies depending on our personality and the positive or negative influence we have received during our lives. This is why one person cannot always pick up on another person's signals, words and thoughts, as they are not able to meet at the same frequency or wavelength.

When communicating, it is therefore always better to try to receive and/or listen at the frequency at which others speak, write or signal out, rather than listening based only on your own frequency.

When two people meet, they always meet with their own personal radar equipment, and they always scan each other's energy field to establish whether or not they like the other person. Subsequently they seek approval from the counterpart to establish if the other person reminds them of someone else they know or used to know.

The signalling, and how the signalling is received, is always huge when two people meet for the first time - and if there are others present at the same time, who have not met previously, the air is full of in and out-going signals among the people present, particularly if there is a specific purpose of the meeting where the parties wish to gain something productive from the time they spend together. In that case verbal communication must take over pretty quickly in order to control the visible signalling, while the invisible signalling continues under the surface.

In a relationship you often depend on open signalling at many levels if the couple wishes to have presence and understanding in relation to one another. If one party chooses to stop the signalling by putting up an invisible wall in the aura, this often creates problems in the couple's communication with each other. When people go their separate ways, it is often because one party feels that the other party's invisible wall in the aura is much too high or thick for him or her to spend any more resources trying to force it. The other party may have no intention of changing his or her way of thinking, feeling and/or acting, which may have contributed to creating the high wall in the person's aura. It is therefore often much easier for the first party to enter into the world to find a new partner where there is more balance in the relationship right from the beginning.

There is hardly ever any reason to start up at the most difficult end of the scale. Instead, start out by doing something that gives you the greatest chance of succeeding right away, as this provides you with the energy to tackle potential challenges later on in the relationship and in life.

POSTSCRIPT

It is not hard to imagine that it must have crucial consequences for Earth as a whole, and for societies around the world, that many spiritually conscious Crystal Children are being born these days with as much focus on the wholeness as on the individual. Also, fortunately for Crystal Children, the Indigos were already here to shake things up, which is why the balance will gradually occur in those places in society where people are on a par with the New Time Energy.

Wherever the energy has yet to be upgraded, there will continue to be trouble and riots until such times as the Crystal Children become adults and together change conditions such that a more balanced way of being, based on their synchronized spiritual/physical convictions, is achieved.

In reality we have already experienced the worst problems that we as humans possibly can during the development era of the Earth, such as death, destruction, natural disasters, war and evil acts being perpetrated between people, etc. - things that have all been experienced by societies in the past. However, many people on Earth do not realize that there are indeed good, sustainable solutions to all problems. It is a prerequisite though that all people are prepared to live in accordance with those solutions and that they understand them. Unfortunately this is a task that the Soul Energy did not successfully manage to achieve through the previous earthly reincarnation system.

Unfortunately, many people have experienced things in their lives through the Soul-controlled earthly reincarnation system, where the lesson to be learned was not made visible until perhaps other and later lifetimes, and completely out of context with the original experiences. Therefore it took much too long for Soul Humans to become insightful, simply because a veil of oblivion descended upon their consciousness when they were reincarnated in a new body.

Therefore, they did not know that they were born time and again on this Earth and that their many lives were closely connected at Soul level where all their actions, thoughts and emotions of the 1st-3rd dimensions were brought into the spiritual Akasha archive, in order to create a general correlation between their many Soul incarnations here on Earth. That is why it took far too long for them to learn from their mistakes so that they could transform their knowledge into something positive for the good of all.

That is why around the turn of the second millennium the Moon, which is home to the Soul Energy and responsible for the reincarnation system, said its partially-prepared goodbye and withdrew its consciousness energy from the Earth, although the physical Moon is still clearly visible in the sky of the Earth. This made room for Jupiter's spiritually and physically transforming Indigo Energy, and subsequently Venus will take over control of the Earth with its spiritually based balancing energy in 2012.

For those already at Indigo level, but especially in the coming Crystal Period, it is possible for people of the New Time to learn from their own mistakes at a very high speed, after which they can start to teach others from the lessons they have learned as a continuation of their own learning. In the Jupiter Energy (as well as the Venus Energy) it is not a question of having had many years of experience or seniority to hold a certain office in society. If you were born to hold a particular office, that is because this is your life mission deep down at cell level and you naturally have all the qualifications required for carrying out your particular assignment.

In the auspices of Venus, people have great respect for all kinds of intelligence that have a pure, visible, spiritual and physical vibration and that support any positive development with a divine spark. Spirit and matter are two sides of the same coin and the Venus-Crystal Energy prefers transparency in every process that can contribute towards understanding and cooperation. Furthermore, physical age is of no consequence with regard to how much, or how little, respect someone can expect from his or her environment. Sometimes, it is merely professional and personal qualifications that determine the degree to which the environment tips their hat to acknowledge a fellow human being. These different forms of intelligence and knowledge will save the Earth in the newly initiated Crystal Era, simply because the main problem of the Earth is the lack of insight and knowledge among the planet's population.

It is merely a lack of insight and intelligence that is slowing down the population of the Earth in their aim to change their consciousness in a positive direction, as not everybody understands the overall plan for the planet. That is why they do not know where to place themselves within the Earth matrix, in order to contribute and thoroughly enjoy the relationship between the wholeness and themselves. In this case an AuraTransformation™ can help most earth focussed people, regardless of their consciousness level prior to the transformation.

In the Venus Energy there is a strong focus on how people's thoughts contribute to shaping their own lives and their relationships with others. You see, people's thoughts act as open and closed doors in the aura and the body respectively, where they affect the degree to which they will each succeed in realizing their life mission and how much inspiration is able to make its way into each person's consciousness, whether professionally or personally. Things will very quickly materialize and become visible if you have an open and balanced approach, as the projects in question will otherwise not be successful. However, it is also possible to consciously focus on keeping certain doors in your system closed if there are certain people or circumstances that for some reason you do not wish to let into your life.

In the Venus Energy, people are also very conscious about the fact that ideas and solutions are on a par with thoughts and actions - two different things that do not automatically belong together, which is what many people at Soul level have made the mistake of thinking. It is therefore good to have nice thoughts, but it is even better to carry those thoughts into life as a specific action, as actions make the absolute difference in the earthly universe.

Spiritually inspired ideas and thoughts therefore represent potential ways to reaching the goal, but the actual movement towards a more physically dense target is the determining leap in connection with people's future consciousness development here on Earth. This is because they need to learn how to get themselves out of their existing living conditions with the help of even the smallest of thoughts and inspiration from within, outside or above as a kind of self-help. By doing things themselves, people learn much quicker, to the benefit both of themselves and their environment. If at the same time they remember to stay focused on thinking only positive and open thoughts, it will become easier for them to get the right inspiration to get on with their lives and their personal, and consciousness, development. It is about seeking the truth and the positive aspects within yourself, even if you do not always know what they are, instead of seeking out various religious, political and ideological centres of force in the outer world, which, unfortunately, seem very attractive to many people because they already form part of the current circumstances and community experience so that many people do not need to make their own opinions about life.

I would like to end this book by introducing you to the following illustration that speaks its own clear language. At the end of the 1990s, this illustration was part of our facilitation material on The Aura Mediator Courses™ and it shows the two opposite energy flows that these days are being brought together as one joint energy in all newborn Crystal Children around the Earth, as well as in all adults who are crystallizing in their aura and body and further into their relationship to the surrounding environment.

For your information, the illustration on the following page is not related to religion.

Thank you for reading!

THE EARTH'S ENERGY STRUCTURE

THE TOTAL CONSCIOUSNESS MASS

With two opposite energies that must be combined in order to create
ORDER and BALANCE in the world

Generally, this represents the West and the East

THE SPIRIT	THE MATTER
The consciousness	The body

THE ENERGY OF CHRIST	THE ENERGY OF BUDDHA

Considers the individual The individual The person	Considers the ideology The religion The wholeness

Conscious about personal needs Can create egoists	Conscious about the structure of society Can create fanatics

"ANNI & THE OTHER STARS"

ABOUT ANNI SENNOV

Anni Sennov was born in 1962 and is the woman behind AuraTransformation™ which since 1996 has gained tremendous ground in Scandinavia and since 2007 has spread into the Baltic countries as well.

She works together with Berit Reaver, who is the director for The Aura Mediator Courses™, and with all other instructors on The Aura Mediator Courses™ in and outside Scandinavia.

Anni Sennov is the author of several books about AuraTransformation™, Crystal Children and Indigo Children, Relationships as well as Energy and Consciousness.

Together with her husband, Carsten Sennov, she is a partner of the publishing company Good Adventures Publishing and the coaching and consulting business SennovPartners where she consults clients on personal development, energy and consciousness.

Together, Anni and Carsten Sennov have developed the Personality Type Indicator four element profile™ that consists of four main energies corresponding to the four elements of Fire, Water, Earth and Air, which are each represented in all people in a variety of combinations of balance and strength.

Anni Sennov originally began her career in the financial world and has run her own practice, firstly with astrological counselling and healing, and then AuraTransformation™ and clairvoyance since 1993.

Anni is very direct and honest, which since 1993 has benefited her clients, the audiences who attend her presentations, as well as her readers - and she is good at giving her clients a kick in the rear, both personally and professionally.

Anni Sennov's work and books have been mentioned in numerous magazines, newspapers and on TV in Denmark, Norway and Estonia.

You can link to Anni Sennov's profile on Facebook, Plaxo, and LinkedIn and subscribe to her newsletter at **www.annisennov.eu**.

Read more at **www.annisennov.eu**

Websites that represent Anni Sennov:

www.annisennov.eu/.dk
www.good-adventures.com/.dk
www.sennovpartners.eu/.dk
www.fourelementprofile.eu/.dk
www.auratransformation.eu/.com/co.uk/.dk/.no/.se/.fi/.co.ee/.ru/.pl/.de/
.at/.ch

Anni Sennov's authorship

Translated into other languages:

The Little Energy Guide 1 - co-author: Carsten Sennov (English)
Den lille energiguide 1 - co-author: Carsten Sennov (Danish)
Den lille energiguiden 1 - co-author: Carsten Sennov (Norwegian)
Den lilla energiguiden 1 - co-author: Carsten Sennov (Swedish)
Väike energia teejuht 1 - co-author: Carsten Sennov (Estonian)

The Crystal Human and the Crystallization Process Part I (English)
The Crystal Human and the Crystallization Process Part II (English)
Krystalmennesket & Krystalliseringsprocessen (Danish)

Crystal Children, Indigo Children & Adults of the Future (English)
Krystalbørn, Indigobørn & Fremtidens voksne (Danish)
Kristallbarn, indigobarn och framtidens vuxna (Swedish)
Kristall-lapsed, indigolapsed ja uue ajastu täiskasvanud (Estonian)
Кристальные дети,дети Индигои взрослые нового времени (Russian)

E-book:

Crystal Children, Indigo Children & Adults of the Future (English)

Current books available in Danish only:

Balance at All Levels (Balance på alle planer)
The Planet Energies Behind the Earth's Population 2005 (Planetenergierne bag Jordens befolkning 2005)

Co-author of:

The Conscious Leader (Den Bevidste Leder - currently available in Danish only) - main author: Carsten Sennov

Free e-book (currently available in Danish only):

Spirit Mates - The New Time Relationship (Åndsdualitet - Den Nye Tids parforhold) - co-author: Carsten Sennov

Sold-out titles (available in Danish only):

Karma-free in the New Time (Karma-fri i den nye tid)

Sold-out titles under the name Anni Kristoffersen (available in Danish only):

Spirit Mates - A Book About Love (Åndsdualitet - en bog om kærlighed) co-author: Carsten Sennov
The New Aura (Den nye aura)
The Planet Energies Behind the Earth's Population (Planetenergierne bag Jordens befolkning)
How Difficult Can It Be? (Hvor svært kan det være?)
The ABC of the Aura Transformation (AURA-ændringens ABC)
Masculine & Feminine Energies (Maskulin & Feminin)
Karma-free and in Harmony (Karma-fri og i harmoni!)
Daily Spiritual Energy (Åndelig energi idagligdagen)
Spiritual Energy (Åndelig energi)

Read more at **www.good-adventures.com**

Related books

The Crystal Human and the Crystallization Process Part I
by Anni Sennov

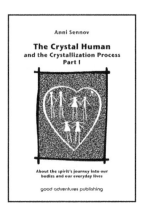

Crystal Children, Indigo Children & Adults of the Future
by Anni Sennov

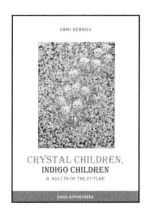

The Little Energy Guide 1
by Anni & Carsten Sennov

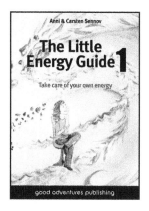

See www.good-adventures.com

Lightning Source UK Ltd.
Milton Keynes UK
UKOW05f1921020317
295772UK00020B/996/P